MUSIC IN THE LIFE OF THE AFRICAN CHURCH

MUSIC IN THE LIFE OF THE AFRICAN CHURCH

Roberta King

with
Jean Ngoya Kidula, James R. Krabill, and Thomas A. Oduro

BAYLOR UNIVERSITY PRESS

Scripture quotations are from the *New Revised Standard Version Bible,*
copyright 1989, Division of Christian Education of the National
Council of the Churches of Christ in the United States of America.
Used by permission. All rights reserved.

Cover Design by Cynthia Dunne; Cover Photo by Stanley Green.
Book Design by Ellen Condict
All photos were provided by the authors.

The following hymns have been used by permission:
 Hustad, Donald P. 1993. "Come to Jesus," chap. 2, p. 226. In *Jubilate
 II: Church Music in Worship and Renewal.* Carol Stream, Ill.: Hope
 Publishing Co. Used by permission of Hope Publishing Co.
 Kidula, Jean Ngoya. 1998. "When You Are Tested," p. 175. In "Sing
 and Shine: Religious Popular Music in Kenya." Ph.D. Dissertation,
 University of California, Los Angeles. Used by permission of the
 author.
 Krabill, James, R. 1995. *The Hymnody of the Harrist Church Among
 the Dida of South-Central Ivory Coast (1913–1949).* 92 vols. Vol.
 74. Frankfurt am Main: Peter Lang. Used by permission of the
 author.

Library of Congress Cataloging-in-Publication Data

King, Roberta Rose, 1949-
 Music in the life of the African church / Roberta R. King with Jean
Ngoya Kidula, James R. Krabill, and Thomas Oduro.
  p. cm.
 Includes bibliographical references (p.) and index.
 ISBN 978-1-60258-022-0 (pbk. : alk. paper)
 1. Church music--Africa. I. Kidula, Jean Ngoya. II. Krabill, James R.
III. Oduro, Thomas, 1955- IV. Title.

ML3051.A37K56 2008
264'.2096--dc22
                                   2007046037

To the unsung heroes of the African church who have put their faith to music and led in singing this faith to their peoples.

Contents

Illustrations

Preface

Music in the Life of the African Church seeks to energize conversations between music, culture, and the church. After more than 500 years between the first encounter of Western Christianity and African traditional religion south of the Sahara, the African church continues to grapple with questions and issues surrounding culture and music in profound ways. One of the major characteristics of African Christianity today is the emergence of culturally appropriate music that has breathed vitality into the life of the church, both in people as witnesses and as present at worship. This has come about at a time when scholars are recognizing the phenomenal growth of the church in Africa in the twentieth century and beyond. They note that, "From an estimated 4 million professing Christians in 1900 African Christianity has grown to over 300 million adherents by the year 2000" (Shaw 2000, 37). This widespread growth is making front page news, especially because the church's unabated growth means that there is a major shift of Christianity into the southern hemisphere (see Jenkins 2002). One of the untold stories of the church's phenomenal growth is the central role of music and its dynamic interaction with African cultures, which is the topic of this book.

The story of music in the life of the African church reveals the central role that different cultural music can, and often does, play in effectively bringing the good news of Jesus Christ into new contexts. It identifies struggles, tensions, and issues that arise when people of differing cultures encounter one another. Such struggles and issues are not limited to Africa alone but are regularly encountered in today's global world because missions in the church continue to introduce new people to Jesus Christ. Music is always linked to cultural contexts. Historically, Western Christianity has not adequately recognized this. Even though music has always played a significant role in the life of the Western church, recognizing the validity of indigenous music found around the world has largely been ignored, which has resulted in wholesale rejection of cultural music. Understanding music as cultural expressions and identity markers is new to the Western church in the twenty-first century, but it is absolutely essential. Thus this work not only tells the story about music in the African church but also brings to light critical issues and insights from African church music that are relevant to the universal church in both global and local contexts.

The global church needs to continually strive to make the gospel more relevant to particular cultural contexts in ways that encourage authentic interaction with the living God. This work seeks to raise categories and paradigms for the church in going about its task of sharing the gospel cross-culturally and living in Christian fellowship as it relates to music. Such highly complex tasks require a forging of new academic and theological links. This study brings together the disciplines of ethnomusicology, theology, and missiology in a unique way, creating a new paradigm that provides lenses for examining music in relation to culture, theology, spirituality, and the church. Although the book is based on our African experience, we believe there are principles and values that apply to any number of worldwide contexts. We address such questions as:

1. How do culture and worldview shape African music?

2. What is music in African cultural life?

3. What was the music culture that Western missionaries brought with them to Africa?

4. What happens to music when people of differing cultures encounter one another?

5. How has music in the African church developed?

6. What processes of contextualization has music undergone to make it meaningful to the people of Africa?

7. How is African Christian music informed and nourished by the scriptures?

8. What are the lessons and principles gleaned from the African church that foster strong and vital faith communities both in Africa and the global church today?

Music in the Life of the African Church is in no way meant to serve as an encyclopedia documenting music in every African church or culture. Rather, we have chosen to recount this untold story in an illustrative way with the goal of stimulating further reflection and conversation about the central role of music in the global church. This volume is not meant to be comprehensive. The African continent and church are too vast and remain beyond the scope of this volume. Although we acknowledge centuries of active interaction with the Christian faith on the African continent, our primary focus is on what has transpired during the last 150 years. Furthermore, we concentrate on sub-Saharan Africa and do not attempt to treat the realities of Christian communities in North Africa, such as the Coptic Church or various forms of Orthodox Christianity. Likewise, what is occurring between Christianity and Islam, Hinduism and various Eastern religions on the African continent would make for a fascinating and much needed area of research, but it is beyond the scope of this study.

Readers will soon note that our bibliographic references are drawn mainly from French and English sources; we have not drawn on materials in Portuguese that describe the church in Lusophone Africa. Our main concern was to find literature that examines the interface between the various aspects of church life and music. Unique to this work is the fact that much of our material is drawn from extensive research, fieldwork, and ministry that we each bring to the text. Each of us has more than twenty years of ministry experience in Africa, which is in addition to visits and other assignments in multiple locations across the continent. Thus we each draw from our experiences as broadly as possible—more particularly from where we have lived and traveled—predominantly in East, Central, and West Africa. Resulting from the desire to keep the volume limited in size and accessible to many and recognizing that there is a considerable amount of literature on music in the southern part of the continent already, we have not attempted to include southern Africa as a major focus. That is also a wonderful story of music in the life of church, but it is one that is not adequately covered in this work. The current volume, nonetheless, makes a major contribution to studies in music, culture, and mission in relation to the church in both global and local contexts, which is an emerging subject that has suffered from a scarcity of materials.

Finally, *Music in the Life of the African Church* is written as a textbook that will serve as a valuable resource for seminary, Bible school, and Christian university students, church leaders, church musicians, worship leaders, missionaries, and those churches desiring to appreciate, value, and incorporate diverse cultural groups into their worship life. With its unique focus on music and its dynamic interaction with culture, the church in mission, biblical theology, and individuals within their cultural context, this volume is intended for those who have a passion for spreading what God has done in ways that dynamically energize the church. For as the psalmist declares, "All the nations you have made will come and worship before you, O Lord; they will bring glory to your name" (Ps 86:9). God is at work among the nations of Africa. They are bringing their worship to Yahweh, the creator God they have longed to know, and they are doing much of it through their music. We invite you to join us on this amazing journey of faith and grace.

Roberta R. King
Jean Ngoya Kidula
James R. Krabill
Thomas Oduro

Acknowledgments

"It takes two hands to play a drum!" This well-known West African proverb highlights the importance of collaboration by expressing that nothing can be done without the help of others. Many people have played critical roles in seeing this volume come to fruition. For this we are extremely grateful and want to acknowledge the following institutions and people:

- Fuller Theological Seminary for recognizing the theological importance of understanding the relationship between music, culture, and God's word by making room for an ethnomusicologist on the faculty.

- Douglas C. McConnell, Dean of the School of Intercultural Studies, who realizes and supports the importance of culturally appropriate music for worship and witness.

- The Brehm Center for Worship, Theology, and the Arts that sponsored multiple meetings of the writing team on Fuller Seminary's Pasadena campus.

- John Witliet, Joel Carpenter, and Michael Hawn for their encouragement to continue in getting this work published.

- Stanley Green, Diane Stinton, and Karen Campbell for providing photos.

- Scott Sternberg, Jeff Simons, and Oksana Bevz, staff members at Fuller Theological Seminary, for their help in bringing the materials together.

- Baylor University Press for catching the vision for making known God's marvelous work among the nations through this publication.

1

Beginnings
Music in the African Church

Roberta R. King

Birds of different rivers chatter differently.
—Ethiopian Proverb, *Amharic*[1]

The dawn chorus sung by local birds on the African continent is glorious. Indeed, the rich variety and diversity of birds are staggering and immense. The birds' songs faithfully greet the new day with each rising of the sun. From the African fish eagle, flamingos, pied king-fishers, and weaverbirds on the shores of Lake Naivasha in Kenya to the contrasting cries of multicolored turacos and West African fish eagles along the river Comoe of Côte d'Ivoire,[2] each unique voice contributes to a grand and glorious doxology proclaiming God's glory. Their lively songs permeate the air. Indeed, they cannot be silenced as they create the local soundscape of their environment.

The birds of each river have their own unique chatter, or sound environment, as our Ethiopian proverb teaches. Yet their purpose is the same; they are each singing of life in their own context. This is also true of the African church and its music. The variety and diversity of music praising God in Africa are as rich and varied as the birds' songs. In profound ways, African church music reveals the life of Christian faith communities within their unique contexts, which are communities of believers seeking to know and understand who Jesus Christ is within their local setting.

MUSIC SCENES IN THE AFRICAN CHURCH

Music in the life of the African church is varied and highly diverse. Though there are many common elements, each local church generates its unique set of church dynamics. No one setting adequately describes music in the church. To begin to grasp the richness of music in the African church in light of the current global era, two musical vignettes provide illustrative windows on the myriad ways in which African peoples interact musically with their Christian faith.

Scene 1: Worship in the City, East Africa

It is a Sunday morning in August 2003. Numerous *Pajeros* and *Mercedes*—high end four-wheel drive and luxury vehicles—surround the Anglican Cathedral in Kampala, Uganda. Parking on the hill is difficult to find. The second of three services is about to begin; already there is standing room only. National leaders and university students rush to find their places. They crowd into the tightly filled sanctuary where many people are standing shoulder-to-shoulder. The sound system is at full volume, and electric guitars wail. An imported pipe organ, a robed choir, and the praise team join together to sing their songs of praise.

1.1 Nairobi Pentecostal Church on Valley Road. The church experienced explosive growth in the 1990s.

The music worship team draws from the multiple streams of their heritage. The history of Christianity in Uganda is filled with martyrdom and civil strife since its initial founding by the Church Missionary Society in 1877. Because of its Anglican roots, the church knows many Western hymns, singing them with great conviction and passion. However they are not restricted to the hymns. The singing of local *pambio* (choruses) and contemporary Christian songs from the West engenders a fuller engagement by the congregation, members singing in their own vernacular tongues and musical languages. Ululations, shrills, laughter, and moving together in body rhythms become the climax of worship before the God who offers hope in the midst of the day's unsettling issues of human immunodeficiency virus (HIV), acquired immune deficiency syndrome (AIDS), and continued war fronts.

Part of the membership includes a group of young professionals, known as the Anglican Youth Fellowship, who have set before them the goals of worship renewal, recreating the Anglican liturgy anew, choosing to sing where the liturgy was once merely read aloud, and composing songs drawn from their African heritage. The freedom to worship in ways that profoundly communicate the work of God in their lives nourishes and strengthens them for the tasks before them. Though their church heritage is the hymns, they love to be "taken home" as they sing songs drawn from their cultural roots. Only then is their music in worship complete.

Scene 2: Worship in the Village, West Africa

Sunday morning worship takes place under the mango trees in a northern Côte d'Ivoire village. The small group of Nyarafolo believers is hearing the story of Abraham for the first time in their mother tongue and set to their vernacular musical style. The story is not recited verbally but is sung in the complex patterns of call-and-response so typical of narrative songs of the Senufo peoples to which the Nyarafolos belong. Neighbors to the Nyarafolos, Cebaara believers have been singing the Christian message for more than thirty years. Although they speak closely related languages, nonbelieving Nyarafolos have long misunderstood the songs sung in the Cebaara language. They misinterpreted them as meaning that the God of Cebaara Christian songs was limited only to the Cebaaras since he spoke *their* language. They did not understand that the Christian God of the Cebaaras also desires a relationship with them.

In addition, the tonal differences between the two languages were often in opposition to one another to such a degree that the song texts became nonsensical in the Nyarafolo language. This created even more layers of barriers to understanding the gospel message of the songs. Now as the small group of Nyarafolo believers listen to the story of Abraham sung in their language and musical style, they are amazed at what they are hearing about Yahweh for the very first time. The Christian Nyarafolos who had made the new songs were excited to see the depth of response. They had discovered that each language group requires not only their own Bible translation but also an appropriate Christian song genre that uniquely suits their language and cultural identity.

What are the dynamics at work in each of these scenes located within sub-Saharan Africa? With each setting strikingly different in terms of musical sound and praxis, how do we begin to analyze and observe what is taking place? What are the common themes that emerge for music in the life of the African church? What implications are evoked for the global church at large? This volume speaks to these issues. Reasons for studying music in the life of the church in sub-Saharan Africa abound.

1.2 Nyarafolo-speaking believers of Côte d'Ivoire share in a praise dance with Djimini-speaking believers. Both groups belong to the larger Senufo group.

WHY STUDY MUSIC IN THE LIFE OF THE AFRICAN CHURCH?

Christian music in the life of the worldwide church plays a central role for gathering faith communities in worship and witness. The church in sub-Saharan Africa excels in providing music a prominent place in its life of faith. In addition, the plethora of Christian music greeting the newcomer to Africa is staggeringly rich and diverse in ways that parallel Africa's chattering birds; each possesses its own unique song. Studies of music in the life of the African church suggest new ways to approach musical issues confronting the global church today. The purpose of this volume is to address the following questions and issues.

The Investigation of Critical Issues in Communicating the Gospel Cross-culturally through Music

The goal of effective mission is to make the gospel, that is the message of Jesus Christ, known and understood among the nations (Matt 28; Mark 16) in all cultural contexts and in ways that promote the making of disciples (see Kraft 1991, Smith 1992). One of the greatest imperatives of the twenty-first century is to understand how differing music communicates within varying cultural contexts. Questions and often ill-informed opinions abound in relation to the cultural music of various peoples. In contrast to current opinions that assume all music is readily understood, this volume explores musical systems or music cultures because they vary from context to context. The concern is that each music culture, viewed as capable of embracing the gospel message, speaks in meaningful ways to the people of differing societies. Regardless of location, there is an interactive dynamic between music and cross-cultural mission, including questions for the missional church in the West that need to be addressed. Studying music in the life of the African church allows for reflecting on critical issues surrounding the relevance and acceptance of the gospel as perceived through music. Music in the church either creates barriers or gateways to the Christian faith. In the history of mission, for example, the introduction of foreign Christian music has most often contributed to a truncated understanding of the gospel. Thus the development of culturally appropriate and authentic music for local churches is of critical importance in fostering Christian faith. One of the goals of this volume is to highlight issues and guidelines that promote the creation of authentic music for worship in spirit and truth (John 4), which foster making Jesus Christ known and worshiped in ways that are understood. The missional question, how can the gospel be communicated cross-culturally in meaningful ways through music, is addressed.

Energizing Conversations among Music, Culture, and the Church

The African church has long grappled with questions and issues surrounding culture and music. Studies in bringing the gospel message to Africa continue to dominate the church's agenda. Christian mission of the nineteenth century encountered a vast array of music traditions, and in essence, did not know how to respond. Missions lacked tools and theory for dealing with the dynamic link between music and culture. The church failed to adequately address critical life-giving issues. This often resulted in schism within the churches.[3] Today, questions and issues surrounding an understanding of music and culture for purposes of the church remain at the forefront of the church's agenda, both in Africa and worldwide. Drawing from the disciplines of ethnomusicology[4] and missiology,[5] the critical questions confronting the global church today must be analyzed and addressed.

Documenting the Story of Music in the Life of the African Church

After more than 500 years since the first encounter between Western Christianity and African traditional religion, the church in sub-Saharan Africa possesses an immense and highly complex history. Music has always played a central role in facilitating life on the African continent. Although studies in world music and ethnomusicology have opened doors to incorporating the West African *djembe* (an open-ended hand drum shaped like a goblet) into church worship in the West, the acceptance of, or development of, African music for worship and witness has not been without its difficulties. What are the issues that arise out of the coming of the Christian faith into new contexts or cultural settings? With Africa's rich history of music in the church, both positive and negative aspects of music's role in making Jesus Christ known among the nations are investigated. What happens to music when different people meet? This study seeks to identify critical arenas of study that need to be addressed when studying church music locally in Africa and in the church globally.

Understanding How African Christian Faith Is a Sung Faith

Studies in church music in the life of the African church also contribute significantly to understanding the Christian faith in the global south. For most of the thousands of churches located in sub-Saharan Africa, music lies at the center of church life. Indeed, a major distinctive feature of the church in Africa is its expressive means of worship and witness through music and song, dance, and drama. This multiplex of inextricably linked artistic forms serves as a vital means to integrating faith within the lives of African Christians for whom to sing is to theologize (to talk about God),[6] to dance is to witness to his goodness and testify to one's relationship with him, and to dramatize is to make the message clear and understandable. Music is integral to a dynamic church as practiced in Christian faith communities. What are the distinctive characteristics of African church music and their implications for global church music in the twenty-first century?

Studying the Place of Music in the Life of a Church Where There Is Phenomenal Growth

Global Christianity has moved to the southern hemisphere in large numbers. The major movements of God have apparently spread southward where, in sub-Saharan Africa alone, Christians increased in number from 10 million in 1900 to a staggering 360 million in the year 2000 (Jenkins 2002, 4).[7] This growth is projected to continue unabated. Some estimates show more than a doubling of Christian adherents in such countries as Nigeria, the Democratic Republic of Congo, and Ethiopia by the year 2050 (Jenkins 2002, 90). Although churches in Latin America and Asia are also growing at significantly rapid rates, the church in Africa with its long historical interaction with the Christian faith offers a rich means of study in global church music. What are the dynamics related to music that contribute to this staggering growth of the church?

Initiating a Mutually Listening Dialogue between the Church in the North and the Church in the South

In today's global era with mass migrations of people, especially from the southern hemisphere to the northern hemisphere, there is increased need to listen and learn from one another. As the church in the north listens to the stories of the church in the south, and vice versa, both faith communities begin to understand one another and their missional roles. In an age that transmits Christianity in new contexts, there is a need to revisit the fraught matters that often impede any church called to fulfilling the "great commission." Theologians and church leaders are now rightly imploring congregations to take a listening position, pointing out how:

> The churches in the North need to listen to, and understand the issues for preaching the gospel in the contexts of the churches of the South, and be aware of how their actions impinge on other people's societies. The churches of the South also need to listen and understand the changing situations for preaching the gospel in the churches of the North (Jacob 2006, 82).

The church in sub-Saharan Africa is positioned as an emerging leader in "making known among the nations what God has done" (Pss 96:3). Philip Jenkins (2002, 3) suggests that by the year 2025, more than 633 million Christians will live in Africa. Music plays a critical role in the vitality of African church life, yet is a commonly overlooked arena of study. It is essential that the global church learn from the African church and its music praxis.

GEOGRAPHICAL SPACES: AFRICA'S GEOGRAPHICAL IMMENSITY, CULTURAL DIVERSITY, AND RELIGIOUS COMPLEXITY

Africa astounds in geographical size and religio-cultural diversity. It is the second largest continent of the world with 28 million square kilometers of surface area as it straddles the equator (Stone 2000, 2). The Sahara desert prevails in northern Africa, whereas the Kalahari Desert lies in the southern portion. Yet there are tropical regions with vast expanses of grasslands and dense rainforests in the central plateau.

Linguistic Factors

Language serves as a critical factor in the songs and music of Africa. Estimates of indigenous languages range from seven hundred to three thousand. Indeed, languages and ethnicities defy clear numbers, which contributes significantly to the continent's dizzying array of diversity. J. H. Greenberg's seminal classification (1966) identified four distinct language phyla (superfamilies): Afroasiatic, Niger-Congo, Nilo-Saharan, and Khoisan.[8] The most prominent

Africa South of the Sahara
LANGUAGE FAMILIES

The Sahara

TROPIC OF CANCER

Arabic

Arabic

Tubu

Tuareg

Fulani Songhai
Wolof
Bambara Mossi   Hausa
Gur
Fon
Akan
Ewe Yoruba
Igbo

Kanuri

Kordofanian

Amharic

Somali

Sara

Oromo

Gbaya

Efik Sango
Ewando
Fang

Mongo

Tigrinya

Ganda Luo

EQUATOR

Lingala
Kongo
Luba

Kinyarwanda
Kirundi

Gikuyu

LANGUAGES

- NILO-SAHARAN
- AFRO-ASIATIC
- NIGER-KORDOFANIAN (Including BANTU)
- KHOISAN
- MALAYO-POLYNESIAN

Chokwe

Mbundu

Bemba Swahili

Chichewa

Shona

!Kung

Sotho

Nama

Nguni

Malagasy

1.3 Africa South of the Sahara: Language Families.
Adapted from Middleton 1997, 2:796.

language groups include speakers of Amharic (20 million), Arabic (160 million) in northern Africa, Igbo (17 million), Oromo (14 million), and Yoruba (20 million). Swahili (spoken in East and Central Africa) and Arabic, Persian, and Hausa (of West Africa) function as lingua franca, with more than 30 million speakers of each language. (Middleton 1997, 798). Major non-African languages introduced during the colonial era or through trade further heighten the language complexity. English, French, Portuguese, and Arabic force a majority of people to function in a minimum of three languages. Kenya, for example, has two official national languages (i.e. English and Kiswahili), with each person also speaking a vernacular tongue, such as LuLuyhia or Gikuyu, from among the forty languages indigenous to Kenya.

Communication in Africa is complicated further with a large portion of the population not being literate. Figures for Africa show that more than 158 million adults and 43 million youths remain unable to function in terms of literacy (United Nations Educational, Scientific and Cultural Organization [UNESCO] 2005).This means that they do not read well enough to function in society as literate people. Oral traditions thrive, however, which offers a marvelous constellation of art forms for meaningful communication of significant messages; songs, proverbs, drama, and dance dominate the communication forms employed in the major life event rituals. Whether highly schooled or limited in reading ability, oral tradition—including music—functions at the core of African societies as a prominent mode of communication. In mostly nonliterate societies, orality dominates the transmission of information, serving like a daily newspaper. When a new song is sung, for example, other activities stop because people seek to listen to the news—the message being communicated in song. In this way, oral traditions remain strong, vigorous, and essential, forming a common means of dynamic interaction for readers and nonreaders alike.

Religious Factors

Indigenous religious beliefs laid the foundation for a highly religious people. Indigenous religions possess some common themes. In particular, the belief in a high, supreme, and distant creator god dominates African life, providing a natural link for introducing belief in Yahweh, the creator of the universe. However the analogy stops there because intermediate deities become the focus of worship that centers itself on divination and sacrificial offerings. Spirits live in water, trees, rocks, and other places, and these become the beings through whose mediation people maintain contact with the creator god. In African traditions, music is linked with religious practices.

Two major religious influences within Africa are Christianity and Islam. Both have influenced music in their religious practices on the continent. Christianity has influenced indigenous music with the introduction of Western hymns. These hymns have long been accused of silencing indigenous African music as a result of the common connection to spirit worship. However "new religious movements, such as *aladura* groups have skillfully linked Christian religious practices with indigenous ones" (Stone 2000, 5). Yet as renowned ethnomusicologist, Ruth Stone, notes, Christianity is not the only "outside" religion to alter the musical soundscape of Africa. She explains,

> Elsewhere, Islam penetrated the forest region and brought changes to local practices, even as it, too, underwent change [ISLAM IN LIBERIA]. The observance of Ramadan, the month of fasting, was introduced, certain musical practices were banned, and altered indigenous practices remained as compromises. (2000, 5)

With the introduction of the Christian faith in the mid-nineteenth century came a plethora of Catholic, Protestant, and Independent Christian churches. Each had their unique philosophy of sacred music in the church. From Pentecostal worship with highly expressive forms to the Churches of God Indiana that strove to keep Christian worshipers from becoming overly excited (Musumba 1993, 36, 88–89), the range of approaches to music in the church are highly diverse. They find common ground, for the most part, in the incorporation of hymns into their life of faith. Yet responses to translated Western hymns have varied, from outright rejection of the music and its gospel message to highly dynamic and fervent singing. Such contrasting tensions that developed over church music can be described simply as differences between "book music and body music" that is, singing from a hymnal and singing in a way that involves the whole body in dance (Corbitt 2002, 1–6). These contrasts are graphically demonstrated across the continent every Sunday morning as the faithful gather to worship. Despite these obvious differences, there is much more behind initial observations about music in the African church.

Intersecting Spheres of the Gospel, Music, and Culture in Africa

The dynamics at play in the musical scenarios described previously in this chapter reveal the interplay between the Christian faith, music, and culture. They parallel many of the same issues encountered in doing cross-cultural mission. Four intersecting arenas of study serve as a framework for the church that is seeking to know God in worship and witness within its local setting.

Missiologists have identified these arenas of study as the 1) missional context, or local cultural context, 2) the biblical text, 3) the faith community, or local church, and 4) the personal pilgrimage of

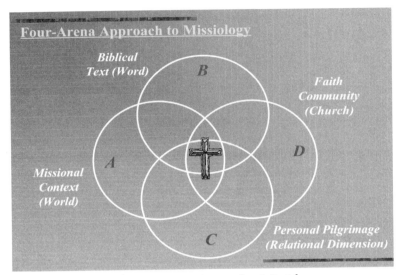

1.4 The Four-Arena Approach to Missiology.
Adapted from Van Engen 2006b, 209.

individuals who belong to the faith community (Van Engen 2006b, 209). This "Four-Arena Approach to Missiology" (see figure 1.4) aids us in fleshing out the Christian faith in the music-making process. In general, "Each domain is a sphere of knowledge, influence, activity and relationships" (Van Engen 2006b, 207). When brought together they form a complex web of dynamic interaction that aids us in unpacking the complex realities at work when sharing the gospel. Furthermore, as Van Engen posits, the centrality of Jesus Christ in all four of the domains provides the overriding, pervasive theme in mission. When music is brought into the equation, a matrix for understanding the multiplex of dynamics at work in global church music emerges: one where the centrality of Jesus Christ is the overarching theme in assessing and developing culturally appropriate Christian music for the church. In this volume, the multiplex of dynamics are applied to the African church. Thus the framework of the matrix provides for musical investigation into each of the four arenas and fosters identification of critical issues, both positive and negative, that impact the life of the church in Africa, and by extension, the global church. In essence, this volume addresses how each of the four components contributes to, and creates, authentic African music for the church.

Briefly, these four domains and their relationship to music in the church can be understood as follows.

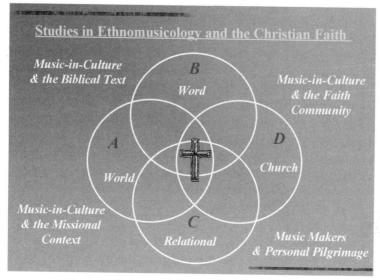

1.5 A Matrix for Studies in Global Church Music.
(Studies in Ethnomusicology and the Christian Faith).

The Missional Context (World)

The missional context makes up the cultural setting in which mission and ministry takes place. Ethnomusicology, the study of music and culture, directly addresses the missional context in relation to music (King 1999b, 327–28). What are the questions about music that need to be asked in African contexts? Each ethno-linguistic group of people not only has their own vernacular language, but they also have their own musical culture through which they find their unique identity. It is imperative, therefore, to be slow to evaluate or judge any people's music without research. One should first seek to understand a people's music. Thus in this domain, it is important to learn to make sense of a people's music found in a particular local context "in terms of both sound and behavior" (King 2004, 296). This arena of investigation, in particular, studies "music-in-culture" and "music in the context of human life" in which each local music is given equal regard and understood on its own terms (Merriam 1964, 32–33). Such study aids in understanding contrasts and differences between musical styles and praxis from the insiders' perspectives. For example, Anglicans in Kampala (Scene 1) are observed singing hymns, contemporary Christian songs, and in their longing to draw from their musical heritage, they are incorporating newly composed African Christian songs into their worship. Nyarafolo-speaking believers in the village setting (Scene 2), on the other hand, make sense of Christian songs only when presented in their indigenous musical style and vernacular language. Both musical approaches are valid and dependent on their unique context because each has its own musical language.

Thus in this arena the following questions emerge about each people's music, or what ethnomusicologists call, music cultures:

1. How is music defined for each cultural group?

2. What is "a group's total involvement with music: ideas, actions, institutions, and material objects—everything that has to do with music" (Titon 2002, 3–32)?

3. How is music used? How does music function?

4. What does the music mean within its own context?

WHAT IS A MUSIC CULTURE?

Travel around the globe or surf the internet and you will encounter a multitude of different musical sounds, instruments, and performance practices. Ethnomusicologists have come to understand that each human society has music unique to its own context. However, these musics are not universally understood. A mission professor once demonstrated an African song of praise in the seminary classroom. Before he could explain its significance, a Korean student asked if it was funeral music. The African song did not mean the same thing to the student. The term *music-culture* provides a means of understanding all the various components of music making that combine to function in meaningful ways within a cultural context. It allows us to learn about different musics of the world in order to understand them from within a people's cultural perspective. It also helps us avoid imposing outside and often false perceptions about a people's music. Music-culture refers not only to musical sounds and styles, but looks at a people's total involvement with music. Key components of a music culture are:
   1) a group's ideas about music,
   2) activities involving music,
   3) repertories of music that include style, genres, texts, composition, transmission, and movement, and
   4) the material aspects of music such as instruments, hymnbooks, musical scores, written documents, clothing (i.e. choir robes), and electronic media equipment. For more information see Titon, 2002.

Biblical Text (Word)

The Scriptures are central to meaningful and truthful communication of the gospel via music. The Scriptures provide us not only with a study of God making himself known in the cultures of the world, but they also serve to inform, shape, and critique the other three domains (Van Engen 2006b, 206). Here key issues in how the church in Africa interacts with the Scriptures as revealed in song will be addressed. How does the church in Africa practice a theology of music-in-context and in what ways does it theologize through the music-making process? The biblical text serves to teach, correct, and nourish in the daily lives of people; a major means of doing so is through song. The singing of the biblical text is central to the spiritual life of the church in Africa.

Personal Pilgrimage (Relational Dimension)

The spiritual pilgrimage, or relational dimension, addresses "the study of *people* making music" (Titon 2002, xiii, italics in original). It considers those who minister through music within the cultural and missional context. Music makers and song leaders in Africa play pivotal roles in bearing "witness to God's love as revealed to us in Jesus Christ" and often serve as instruments of "ongoing transformation in the world" (Shenk 1999, 59), especially when related to inherent cultural music concepts and practices. In this arena of investigation, we reflect on critical qualities and skill sets of musicians in the church and their influential roles as leaders assigned through cultural norms.

Faith Community (The Missional Church)

In this final arena, we come full circle in reflecting on the church in its missional task. This is the arena wherein the ways in which music actively participates in the goal of making Jesus Christ known and worshiped among the nations are investigated. Music making provides a means for the *doing* of mission and ministry; it plays critical roles in worship, witness, spiritual formation, and leadership. Music dominates African church life. It excels in communicating the gospel through its high participation value and prominence at church events and in the liturgy. In this section, guidelines for developing indigenous songs, issues in incorporating local instruments into church music, and approaches to contextualizing worship and liturgy are identified.

What then is music in the life of the church in sub-Saharan Africa? In many ways, it is a story of God at work among the nations through music. To understand that story demands investigating the historical church music that Euro-American missionaries took with them as they journeyed onto a new continent. Chapter 2 explores the question, "What was the Euro-American musical culture of the nineteenth century that accompanied the introduction of Christianity into sub-Saharan Africa?"

FOR DISCUSSION

1. Why is it important to research and to understand a people's music?

2. Share stories with one another about how music forms barriers or creates gateways to (a) receiving a message, (b) receiving a Christian message, (c) worship in the church, and (d) Christian witness.

3. In your opinion, what are the two most important reasons for studying music in the life of the African church? Explain.

4. How is music used in your church? In your local community events? Use the four domains (fig. 1.5) for studying global church music to analyze music in the life of your church and local community.

5. CLASS PROJECT: We live in a global era in which people from around the world are working and worshiping alongside one another. Make a survey of the different ethnic churches that worship in your local city or town. How many of them are African? Attend one of their worship services, and identify as many ways as possible that music works in the life of their church.

2

Music Culture
Euro-American Christianity

Roberta R. King

Sounds are the breathing airs of the heart.

—Kenyan Proverb[1]

As the woman arrived back on Kenyan soil and walked into the Moi International Airport, the contrast between West and East Africa struck her in the face. Walking through the hallways to the immigration desk, the Western missionary proudly carried her newly acquired 17-key wood-framed Senufo xylophone (balafon).[2] Yet over the loud speaker came the strains of the Swedish hymn, "How Great Thou Art," performed as a four-part choral anthem sung in the Kiswahili language accompanied by an electronic keyboard. Having just completed six months of research among Senufo Christians in the north of Côte d'Ivoire where translated Western hymns had failed miserably, the challenges and richness of African musical traditions dominated her thoughts. Yet here she was, back in East Africa where the Christian message had been proclaimed for more than 150 years. It was striking that Euro-American hymns had become so totally embedded in the local soundscape that they could be heard, not only in church, but also in public places, including the bank.

The following week the missionary woman was asked to play a piano solo for the women's fellowship at Nairobi Baptist Church. Excited about her discoveries in the music of Africa and pleased with herself that she had learned to play a traditional African instrument, she chose to perform on her balafon instead. Afterward, one of the leaders asked how she could obtain a balafon from Côte d'Ivoire. She

*explained, "I never knew we could play one of our own African instru-
ments in church. We were taught that it could only be the piano."
Surprisingly, the missionary had not realized how deeply the association of Christianity with Euro-American music ran. She began asking
anew: What was the history of church music in sub-Saharan Africa
that she had inadvertently played into? . . . By the way, I was that
woman.*

2.1 *Senufo balafons are wood-frame xylophones and are shown here being
played in interlocking fashion between the players in Ferkessedougou,
Republic of Côte d'Ivoire.*

Missionary hymns from both Europe and the United States are prolific in large portions of the church in sub-Saharan Africa today. They
form a foundational core of the church's worship heritage across
the continent, especially within mission-founded churches.[3] Ever
since 1482, when the first Catholic masses were said in Portuguese
in Guinea and Ghana (in West Africa), external musical influences
have formed mainstays within the Christian church. Sacred music
and mission have functioned hand in hand. Scholars inform us that:

> [b]eginning in the sixteenth century, Spanish, French, and English
> missionaries used their sacred songs strategically to capture the
> attention and loyalty of those they hoped to win to the gospel of
> Christ. (Stowe 2004, 117)

The sixteenth century was not the exception, however. Across the centuries, missionaries brought their practices of spirituality and worship with them. For example, the White Fathers and the Benedictines introduced Gregorian chant into the liturgy in Tanzania, East Africa in the nineteenth century (Hastings 1994, 257; Mbunga 1963, 19). The chant met with a satisfactory reaction as a result of its remarkable affinities with African music, in particular its modal settings and call-and-response form. As with most missionaries, there was little to no understanding that the Africans had their own genuine religious music.

Rather than using indigenous instruments, missionaries introduced their own, which led African musicians to change their style of playing that sounded neither African nor European. Africans commented that "When the white people hear it they think it is African, and when we hear it we think it is European" (Mbunga 1963, 21). The mass and its liturgical music were performed in Latin with no changes coming before the Second Vatican Council in 1963. After that time adaptation of the liturgy, incorporating African music in the area of hymns and psalmody, became a central concern in Catholic mission (see Murray 1966). Likewise, the Moravian Brethren,

---

Catholic Efforts in Indigenous Hymnody

Stephen B. G. Mbunga (1927–1982), a Tanzanian priest, was among the first Catholics in East Africa to encourage the development of indigenous African church music. Even though the first masses had been said in Latin on the African continent in 1492, nothing happened in relation to indigenous music until the Vatican Council II made it permissable in 1963.

Mbunga pointed out at that time, ". . . we find today patches of various European Church Music in the different missions of Tanzania as are the nationalities of the European Missionaries that brought the Faith. Thus Tanzania started by inheriting more than a single European nationality ever did" (Mbunga 1968, 372). Mbunga wrote prolifically and worked tirelessly for the new air that fostered "baptizing the culture of the country rather than single converts . . . [where] the spirit of indigenous Church Music has now begun to pulsate audibly, and the Church in Tanzania has responded to this spirit by encouraging and harnessing it . . . " (Mbunga 1968, 373).

He was convinced that the more African believers sang their faith in African musical idioms, the more profoundly the faith penetrated their souls (Mbunga 1963, 21).

the first Protestant missionaries to Africa renowned for their deeply spiritual, pietistic practices, continued singing their hymns and liturgy as they arrived in both West and South Africa in 1737. As missions increased during the eighteenth and nineteenth centuries, so did the musical practices transported onto the African continent; people continued to bring "from their places of origin religious belief systems and accompanying musical practices" (Stowe 2004, 226).

The story of Euro-American sacred music is vast and multilayered. The purpose of this chapter is to trace Euro-American music cultures when Protestant churches were initiating missions to Africa, predominantly in the eighteenth and nineteenth centuries. I ask, what was the music of the Europeans and later Americans as they brought the gospel message? What factors existed that fostered a wholesale transplanting of Euro-American Christian music into so many parts of Africa? What were the prevailing ideas or concepts of music, the performance practices, material objects, and musical institutions that first European and later U.S. missionaries introduced as they worshiped with new believers? In other words, as European and U.S. missionaries set sail for Africa to the strains of Isaac Watts's "Jesus Shall Reign Where 'Ere the Sun," what were the music cultures they inevitably transported with them?

REFORMATION ROOTS OF EURO-AMERICAN PROTESTANT MUSIC

The roots of Euro-American Protestant music are grounded in the Protestant Reformation itself. Beginning in the early sixteenth century and considered by many as the greatest renewal movement in Christendom's history, the Protestant Reformation initiated major reforms in worship and music. What emerged were the roots of diverse Protestant faith communities, among them Lutheran, Anglican, and Calvinist-Reformed traditions. Motivated by a common desire to return to biblical authority, *sola scriptura*, and to communicate the scriptures in the vernacular, the music of the European church was profoundly impacted. The Reformation's renewed commitment to the God of the biblical scriptures laid the foundational impetus for new patterns of worship and renewal. Precedents for evangelical Protestant sacred music were firmly established, traces of which continue to impact the African church today.

Martin Luther, the most important German reformer and theologian, considered music a gift of God. Quoting St. Augustine, he implored the church to "see in music your Creator and to praise him through it" (Hustad 1993, 186). Luther welcomed and embraced a wide range of music, from the most sophisticated art forms of his time to the popular folk music traditions in which he participated. Luther's recovery of the doctrine of the priesthood of believers influenced his reforms by fostering a high degree of participation in both worship and song. Not only did Luther translate the Bible into the German vernacular, but he was also a prolific composer, hymn writer, and compiler of the first German hymnal. Musically, Luther's hymns often drew from the cultural songs of the day, setting Christian texts to their melodies. "A Mighty Fortress is our God," based on Psalm 46, is one example. Luther's purpose in hymns was three-fold: "theological (to demonstrate believer-priesthood), liturgical (to retain what he considered orthodox in the Roman mass), and pedagogical (to teach Lutheran doctrine)" (Hustad 1993, 188–89). These principles formed the philosophical roots for the musical innovations incorporated into Lutheran worship and ultimately the Protestant church.

> ### Next to Theology
> ### by Martin Luther
>
> "Next to theology, I give a place to music: for thereby all anger is forgotten, the devil driven away, and melancholy, and many tribulations, and evil thoughts are expelled. It is the best solace for a desponding mind." —Martin Luther (Stowe 2004, 17)

Later in the sixteenth century, additional musical roots emerged. In contrast to Luther, John Calvin took a more restrictive approach to music in worship. Fearful of music's seductive and distracting charms, he discarded both the choir and organ from worship. In their place, he introduced the singing of Psalms in metrical French that led to the *Geneva Psalter*. Sung in unison and without accompaniment by the congregation, the melodies were drawn from a range of sources including French and German secular songs, bits of Gregorian chant, or newly composed tunes. Rhythmically, the songs were dance-like, often derisively called "Geneva Jiggs." Following Calvin's lead, the Anglicans practiced congregational singing of metrical Psalms. Yet they chose to follow Luther's choral lead and brought choral music to a high level. The choir's purposes were twofold. First and foremost, choirs were to lead in congregational singing. Secondly, they were to sing a set piece in the vernacular, which later became known as the choir anthem.

> **HYMN FROM CALVIN'S GENEVA PSALTER**
>
> All people that on earth do dwell,
> sing to the Lord with cheerful voice;
> him serve with joy, his praise forthtell,
> come ye before him and rejoice.
>
> The Lord, ye know, is God indeed;
> without our aid he did us make;
> we are his folk, he doth us feed,
> and for his sheep he doth us take.
>
> O enter then his gates with praise,
> approach with joy his courts unto;
> praise, laud and bless his name always,
> for it is seemly so to do.
>
> For why? The Lord our God is good,
> his mercy is forever sure,
> his truth at all times firmly stood,
> and shall from age to age endure.

Thus the worship and music innovations of the Protestant Reformation fostered bringing the Christian message into the local context of Germany, Switzerland, and England. The contextualization of Christian music revolved around reformation tenets of employing vernacular languages in worship and song and participative congregational singing. Fidelity to the scriptures in hymn texts was paramount, yet Luther and Calvin applied divergent approaches. Throughout the centuries, the roots of Protestant sacred music have remained central to the foundation, yet they have branched out in diversified ways as the gospel has been proclaimed in new communities.

Expanding Branches of Euro-American Sacred Music

Musical innovation in Euro-American sacred music most often appears at times of renewal and revival. Wherever there is a new movement of the Holy Spirit, there is a burgeoning of new song, usually drawn from local folk music styles of the era. Many of Luther's hymns are examples of such outpouring of new song. Significantly, this can also be observed in both Europe and America, especially from the mid-eighteenth through the nineteenth centuries. In particular, continued interaction between Britain and America (Britain's new world colony) fostered the cultural exchange of Christian music that became central to revivalism. As David Stowe notes (2004, 7), "Sacred music flowed rapidly within the Anglophone world at the time of the Awakenings of the mid-1700s and early 1800s, and again after the Civil War."

At the same time, mission work was a growing and prominent force. Lining up the historical flow of mission work against

Euro-American church music traditions reveals a dynamic intersection between the movement of the Holy Spirit in renewal, musical innovations within the Church, and the expansion of the Kingdom of God (see figure 2.2). In the mid-eighteenth and nineteenth centuries when missions were extending into Africa, emerging Euro-American sacred music was making profound spiritual impact within its own local contexts. As new waves of missionaries turned toward Africa, they naturally carried with them the sacred music that was central to their Christian identity. I focus here on pivotal Euro-American faith communities whose Christian music ultimately made its way onto the African continent.

Moravians and the Oxford Group

During the Evangelical Awakening in Britain, a momentous encounter took place in 1735 when two European church groups sailed aboard the same ship to America. United in missional purpose, German-speaking Moravians and English-speaking clergymen from Oxford, among them John and Charles Wesley, began worshiping together. The Moravians had a rich tradition of congregational song-centered worship to which John Wesley was powerfully drawn. The deeply personal and emotional hymns, full of vivid imagery of Christ's atoning blood, appealed to John so much that he translated thirty-three hymns into English during his two-year sojourn in America. The experience profoundly impacted both Wesley brothers. As Methodism began to take shape, John became a strong proponent of congregational song exhorting believers to "Sing all. . . . Sing lustily. . . . Sing modestly . . . sing in time . . . sing

> **A MORAVIAN HYMN**
> (translated by John Wesley)
>
> Jesus, thy Blood and Righteousness
> my beauty are my glorious dress;
> mid flaming worlds, in these arrayed,
> with joy shall I lift up my head.
>
> Bold shall I stand in that great day,
> cleansed and redeemed, no debt to pay;
> for by thy cross absolved I am
> from sin and guilt, from fear and shame.
>
> Lord, I believe thy precious blood,
> which at the mercy seat of God
> pleased for the captives' liberty,
> was also shed in love for me.
>
> Lord, I believe were sinners more
> than sands on the ocean shore,
> thou hast for all a ransom paid,
> for all a full atonement made.

2.2 *Church Music and Mission: Sub-Saharan Africa.*

Church Music and Mission: Sub-Saharan Africa

	Euro-American Church History: Missions to Africa	*Euro-American Sacred Music*
1482	First Masses Said in Guinea and Ghana: Introduction of European Music into Africa	
1500s	**The Protestant Reformation**	
	1517 Martin Luther	-Lutheran Hymns: congregational song
	1562 John Calvin	-Choral anthems
		-Metrical Psalmody
		-Non-Instrumental
		-No Choir
	1549 Anglican Reforms	-Book of Common Prayer introduced
	1562	-"Sternhold and Hopkins" English Psalter
		-Anglican choral anthem emerges
1726–1795	**The Evangelical Awakening in Britain and Great Awakening in the Americas**	
	1735-1736 Moravian emigrants & Wesleys (The Oxford Holy Club) sail to the Americas on the same ship	-Isaac Watts: psalm paraphrases and "hymns of human composing"
	1737 Moravian missionaries arrive in both West and South Africa	-John Wesley learns German from a Moravian hymnbook and translates 33 hymns into English
	1774 John Wesley condemns slavery	
	1784 411 freed slaves leave London for Freetown, Sierra Leone	1780: Wesley publishes worded hymnal: A Collection of Hymns for the Use of the People Called Methodists
	1792 William Carey & Founding of the Baptist Missionary Society; Nova Scotian Methodists to Freetown	-Freed African-American slaves arrive in Freetown singing a Methodist hymn: "Awake and Sing the Song of Moses and the Lamb"
	1795 London Missionary Society Founded	

The Second Great Awakening

1799–1830

- 1799   London Missionary Society sends its first missionaries to the Cape (South Africa)
- 1807   Britain passes bill prohibiting slave trade
- 1816   Ntsikana: a Xhosa chief converts: composes 4 indigenous hymns for his congregation
- 1821   Gambia: Methodist mission work begins
- 1822   Liberia: Baptist mission work begins
- 1828   Ghana: Basel mission work begins
- 1830   Ethiopia: Church Missionary Society begins
- 1833   Slavery legally abolished in the British Empire

- Hymns of Watts and Wesleys continue to form the foundation of Euro-American sacred music

Era of Victorian Hymns in the UK: Estimates of 400,000 Hymns Composed

1837–1901

- 1843   Samuel Ajayi Crowther: Africa's 1st Anglican Bishop
- 1844   Kenya: CMS work begins
- 1847   David Livingston settles in Kolobeng
- 1868   Bagamoyo Tanzania: Catholic mission; Great Lake Region: UMCA, LMS & CMS; Tanzania: German missions

- Multiple hymn collections made
- Robed and surpliced choirs introduced
- Massive pipe organs become common
- 1861: Hymns Ancient and Modern, 1st edition
- 1875: Hymns Ancient and Modern, 2nd edition
- 1889: Supplement to A & M: 176 new hymns

Moody/Sankey: American Revival Team's 1st Tour in Britain, Ireland & Scotland

1873–1875

- 1870   Uganda: CMS begins mission work
- 1877   Uganda: White Fathers begin mission work
- 1879   Kenya: A Presbyterian begins industrial mission
- 1891   Kenya: African Inland Mission founded
- 1895   Nairobi, Kenya – Holy Ghost Fathers begin work
- 1899   Kenya Highlands: CMS begins among Kikuyu
- 1901

- 1870: "Hold the Fort" published as sheet music
- 1873: Sankey publishes gospel song books
- 1875: Sankey publishes Sacred Songs and Solos
- Rise of the folk gospel song
- Gospel hymn develops

World Missionary Conference in Edinburgh

1910

- 1903
- 1930

- Hymns Ancient and Modern: 1,200 hymns
- Rise of traditional gospel

spiritually" (Stowe 2004, 25). His brother, Charles, influenced many lives through the writing of six thousand five hundred hymns that focused on the successive stages in the life of the Christian pilgrim.

Methodism's purpose for hymns mirrored its Protestant Reformation roots; hymns should impart theological knowledge and acquaintance with the scriptures. Hymns served as prayer book, schoolbook, and catechism. The preface to Charles Wesley's published words-only hymnal, *A Collection of Hymns for the Use of the People Called Methodists* (1780), underlines his intention; "So that this book is in effect a little body of experimental and practical divinity" (Marini 2006, 126). The hymnal became an essential medium of doctrinal instruction for Methodists and acquired an inseparable place alongside the Bible because it freely adapted popular tunes so that congregations could easily participate. In 1792, freed African slaves from Nova Scotia arrived in Freetown (Sierra Leone) singing a Methodist hymn, "Awake and Sing the Song of Moses and the Lamb."

The Era of Victorian Hymns: Hymns Ancient and Modern

The era of Victorian hymns perhaps has had the greatest impact on music in the African church. The establishing of missions to Africa in the first half of the eighteenth century continued unabated into the Victorian era. By the second half of the eighteenth century, there was a growing restlessness and abhorrence of slavery. John Wesley's 1794 pamphlet, *The Antislavery Crusade*, condemned slavery and served as a precursor to its abolition in the British Empire in 1833. When Queen Victoria took to the throne in 1837, an unprecedented explosion of hymn writing swept through the Anglican Church and across European evangelical denominations. Hymns became firmly embedded in the socioreligious life of evangelical believers. In mission, for example, historians observe the growing influence of literacy and hymns:

> [T]he 1840s witnessed the penetration of the (African) continent by an army of earnest Protestant missionaries to a degree hitherto unprecedented. . . . What was beginning to make a decisive difference to Africa by 1850 was the diffusion of copies of the New Testament, of hymnbooks, prayer-books, and what have you (including, quite soon, a series of versions of *Pilgrim's Progress*) in a number of important languages." (Hastings 1994, 243)

Despite their lack of sophisticated training in music, missionaries instinctively packed their church's hymnal in their baggage. Only the Bible held a higher place in their spiritual lives. Thus hymns formed a core component in their worship, spirituality, and Christian identity. Although early nineteenth century missionary hymns consisted mostly of "Watts and Wesley" (Hustad 1993, 224), new innovation and reform in congregational song during the Victorian era generated further expansion of Euro-American musical practices. Drawing from Ian Bradley's insightful work (1997), *Abide with Me: The World of Victorian Hymns*, the period expanded Euro-American sacred music in many ways, which are briefly discussed here.

The Prominence of Hymnody in Britain

The unprecedented hymn explosion—some 400,000 hymns written between 1837 and 1901—underscores the Victorians' high regard for hymn writing as a valued vocation. Clergy, poets, academics, classical composers, and numerous distinguished amateurs alike participated. Hymn writing was not left to the music specialist; clergymen in rural Anglican parishes and in urban, city parishes in the Scottish Presbyterian Church contributed the majority of new materials that appeared in Victorian hymnbooks.

Victorians widely recognized the immense power and influence of hymns in communicating theological truth. "Let me write the hymns of a Church and I care not who writes the theology," declared the great Congregational preacher, R. W. Dale (Bradley 1997, 81).

Hymn writing belonged to the church's practice of spirituality. Women, though restricted in other church ministries, enjoyed a welcoming place in writing prominent hymns. Their major contributions lay in the children's sections of hymnals and with collections of songs that came with the emergence of the Sunday school movement in which hymns were intended to educate people on basic doctrines of the faith and to defend creedal orthodoxy.

Significantly, the dominant purpose of Victorian hymnody was to instruct people in faith, rather than to convert, as was the major intent for Watts, the Wesleys, and hymn writers of the Evangelical Revival. Thus it is that great numbers of hymn texts concentrated on exploring central articles of the creed, theological elucidations of the trinity, and attempted to tackle difficult or complex doctrines; for example, Emily Elliott's "Thou Didst Leave Thy Throne and Thy Kingly Crown" that sought to expound the kenotic theory. Death featured as a central theme among the hymns and included frequent

Hymn Writer	Position	Hymn Title
Church of England		
Henry Alford	Vicar	Come ye thankful people come
Henry Baker	Vicar	The King of love my shepherd is
Sabine Baring-Gould	Curate	Onward Christian Soldiers
John Ernest Bode	Rector	O Jesus I have promised
William Walsham How	Rector	For all the saints
Henry Francis Lyte	Perpetual Curate	Abide with me Praise my soul, the King of Heaven
John Mason Neale	Warden	Christ is made the sure foundation
Samuel Stone	Curate	The Church's one foundation
Scottish Presbyterians		
Horatius Bonar	Parish Minister	I heard the voice of Jesus say
Walter Chalmers Smith	Parish Minister	Immortal, invisible, God only wise
George Matheson	Parish Minister	O love that wilt not let me go
Women Authors		
Elizabeth Clephane		Beneath the cross of Jesus
		There were ninety and nine that safely lay
Catherine Hankey		Tell me the old, old story
Frances Havergal		Who is on the Lord's side
		I am trusting thee, Lord Jesus
		Take my life and let it be
Caroline Noel		At the name of Jesus
Mrs. Alexander		All things bright and beautiful
		There is a green hill far away
		Once in royal David's city
		Jesus calls us o'er the tumult

2.3 Popular Hymns and Hymn Writers during the Victorian Era.
Adapted from Bradley 1997.

references to heaven, hell, and judgment. The focus on death reflects the high mortality rate among children of the era and a profound desire to deal theologically and pastorally with it. Embedded in the song texts are critical issues and the stuff of daily life, which was confronting the church at that time and which the hymns earnestly attempted to make theological sense of. The hymns became mechanisms for processing the realities of life.

Hymns for All of Life

The role and use of hymns in Christian life during this period knew no boundaries. Hymns permeated daily life; they were not limited to Sunday mornings or to church buildings. Rather, hymns were sung everywhere—on street corners, at secular meetings, in the nursery, in school rooms, at public meetings and social gatherings, and at home—not just at church and chapel. The Primitive Methodists declared they did not need hymns for public worship only, but also "they need them for the sick chamber, for the marriage feast, for funerals, for journeys by sea and land, for various social gatherings, for the home sanctuary, for personal and private use, for praising the Lord 'secretly among the faithful' as well as in the 'great congregation'" (Bradley 1997, 8). Commonly preferred over parlor ballads and music hall numbers, their texts were cited on postcards and tombstones, on framed posters hung at home, and in school textbooks. In essence, hymns became the dominant folk song of the day and to such an extent, that some church historians acknowledge "the hymn rather than the sermon provides the most characteristic expression of Victorian Christianity" (Bradley 1997, xvi–xvii).

The Growth of Musical Education

The popularity of hymnody coincided with a massive upsurge of interest in teaching proper singing at both school and at the adult level. In reaction to the old regime of gallery bands that played to passive congregations, music educators and clergy strove for cultural improvement and congregational participation. This movement for "correct singing" strove to make singing accessible to all, especially children of all economic levels. By the end of 1841, estimates show more than fifty-thousand working-class children in London were learning to sing from trained vocal teachers (Bradley 1997, 33). Teacher training schools came into prominence because the Church of England placed choral singing at the core of the curriculum. This new burst of popular involvement in choral singing arose out of the conviction that singing would improve the morals of schoolchildren and of the nation. At the same time, the Sunday school movement promoted the habit of singing hymns in profound ways. Children who attended Sunday schools—some three out of every four by 1888—learned to sing, generally by the tonic sol-fa method and additionally enjoyed action songs and dramatized choruses (Bradley

1997, 34). Hymn singing in primary schools, Sunday schools, and at home created a powerful shared oral culture.

Musical Innovations

Musical innovations were numerous during this time, including the introduction of properly trained robed choirs, pipe organs, and simple, more dignified hymn tunes by music educators and clergy. It was the flowering of unprecedented choral singing, both at the parish church level and in the larger cathedrals. The organ became the preferred instrument of praise. Portable harmoniums were introduced, whereas barrel organs[4] replaced gallery bands in English country churches. Congregational churches and Scottish Presbyterians also introduced choirs and organs into their services.

The music philosophy of the era was fourfold. First, the hymns were to be sung in unison, though four-part singing continued. Second, the hymns needed to be easy to sing and accessible to all. The melody was to be clearly marked and not covered by flowery arrangements. Metrical psalms were to be sung with a more controlled, solemn, and reverential sound appropriate to worship. The installation of massive pipe organs contributed to a more "churchy" sound that facilitated dynamic congregational singing.

By far the most significant innovation was the proliferation of hymn collections and the making of hymnals. The practice of singing hymns had become firmly embedded in the services of the Church of England. The singing of Psalms with complex orchestral accompaniment was replaced with new collections of hymns. The British Catalogue of printed books lists over one thousand two hundred hymnals published between 1837 and 1901. The deluge of hymnals culminated in the arrival of *Hymns Ancient and Modern* in 1861. It brought together the proliferation of hymn collections into one book providing order, efficiency, and ease of communication. *Hymns Ancient and Modern* became the most successful hymnal in the Church of England for more than seventy-five years, selling steadily at a rate of three thousand copies a week for thirty-five years. By the end of the century, more than thirty-five million copies had been sold, with sales continuing into the twenty-first century (Bradley 1997, 54–55). Perhaps the most significant feature of the hymnal was the new practice of coupling of specific tunes with hymn texts, a practice that revolutionized the format of hymns.

Ultimately, the making of hymnals remains a distinctive feature of Victorian hymnody. As Bradley explains:

> [f]rom modest origins as a tool of reforming clergy wishing to improve congregational worship, the hymn-book became one of the central institutions of Victorian religion, defining the identity of different denominations and church parties and providing a handbook for doctrine and devotion which, if sales provide any indication, had more influence and impact than any other category of publication." (Bradley 1997, 53)

With the publication of *Hymns Ancient and Modern*, hymns acquired the accepted and respected position that "continued well into the twentieth century in many church groups. Its character, aims, and ideals set the standard for hymnals that followed" (Esker and McElrath 1995, 156–58).

The Rise of Gospel Songs in the United States (and Britain)

Although hymns focusing on Christian living were thriving in Britain, revivalist movements in the United States arose that led to extraordinary influence on the church. In the early nineteenth century, new configurations of churches (i.e., Presbyterians, Baptists, and Methodists), which were intent on evangelism, joined together in frontier camp meetings in which a new type of music appeared. Spiritual songs (Col 3:16) or "spirituals," as they came to be known, were characterized by spontaneous singing, great simplicity, much repetition, and commonly consisted mainly of a chorus. From *The Revivalist* songbook of 1872, we hear:

> Come to Jesus, come to Jesus, Come to Jesus just now,
>
> Just now come to Jesus, Come to Jesus just now.
>
> He will save you, he will save you, He will save you just now,
>
> Just now he will save you, He will save you just now.
>
> (Hustad 1993, 226)

Camp meeting songs were integral to the music training that developed in the American Sunday School Union[5] in 1817. Religious songs for children took on catchy, easily remembered melodies and simple harmonies and rhythms, which always led to a refrain or chorus. These songs combined with Singing Schools

> ### EARLY GOSPEL:
> ### SUNDAY SCHOOL SONGS
>
> - Jesus loves me
> - He leadeth me
> - Sweet hour of prayer
> - Just as I am, without one plea
> - My hope is built on nothing less
> - I am thine, O Lord
> - Jesus, keep me near the cross
> - Pass me not, O gentle Savior
> - Rescue the perishing
> - To God be the glory
> - What a friend we have in Jesus
> - I love to tell the story

and the rise of various evangelistic missions, such as the Young Men's Christian Association (YMCA), led to what is known as gospel songs, or "hymns of experience." Fundamentally, the songs communicated the basic gospel (sin, grace, and redemption) in light of human experience. They became integral in shaping new patterns of evangelism and worship practices that relied on solos and gospel songs to move people toward a relationship with Jesus Christ. Like in England, composers and poets were highly prolific. Fanny Crosby, the blind Methodist teacher, wrote some eight thousand hymn texts, including "All the Way My Savior Leads Me," "Blessed Assurance, Jesus Is Mine," and "Jesus Is Tenderly Calling Thee Home." The outpouring of new Christian music accompanied movements of the spirit and revival.

During the Second Great Awakening, music and revival intersected in new ways. In 1826, Charles Finney, a Presbyterian evangelist, began leading missions in urban centers, such as New York City. Finney relied on a leading music teacher, conductor, and author, Thomas Hastings (1784–1872), during his campaign meetings. At the conclusion of the sermon, songs were used as part of a lengthy, emotional altar call. Thus began the wedding of rational preaching with the emotional appeal of gospel songs. Each evangelist had their distinctive role to play; one preached while the other evangelized through song. Finney's pattern of "planned revivalism" was brought to greater heights through the evangelistic team of Dwight L. Moody (1837–1899) and his soloist-cum-song leader, Ira D. Sankey (1840–1908).

Moody and Sankey became especially famous through their evangelistic missions to Great Britain beginning in 1873. Rallies were held in England, Scotland, and Ireland with great numbers flocking to them; 1.5 million people attended the London rallies. Based on Finney's model, the evangelistic team was made up of an

evangelist and a multitalented musician. Sankey, known for his stir-
ring solos, brought together large, mixed-voice choirs gathered from
local churches that hastily rehearsed before each rally; but above all,
he led in rousing congregational singing. The emotional appeal of
song played a critical role. It was said that:

> Mr. Moody breaks up the fallow ground, and Mr. Sankey's music is
> like an angel's song at the pearly gates, to invite the troubled sinner
> in from the troubles of a perishing world. (Stowe 2004, 97)

Just as hymns were the folk songs of Britain, gospel songs
acquired an equal position in America. "Hold the Fort," the signa-
ture song of Moody and Sankey's mission tour, penetrated music
halls and was whistled by errand boys on the street. Out of this
mission, came the publication of *Sacred Solos and Songs* that grew to
one thousand two hundred songs by 1903. Sales in Britain, close to
eighty million, rivaled those of *Hymns Ancient and Modern* (Wilson-
Dickson 1996, 138).

Most significantly, the success of U.S. gospel songs in Great Britain was perhaps a result of their inherent cultural affinities with
British popular music. As song texts addressed current sociopolitical
issues, the melodies seemed hauntingly familiar. A Glasgow partici-
pant observed:

> [w]ho does not feel the sweetness of Irish melody in 'Sweet by-
> and-by' . . . and the thorough Scottish ring in such songs as 'Hold
> the Fort'. . . . It takes us by surprise to hear gospel truth wafted
> in the strains of our national music; but is it not possible that this
> may be the true though unexpected reason why these simple songs
> have found such a direct and wonderful entrance to the Scottish
> heart? (Stowe 2004, 100)

Although American gospel songs resonated with shared musical
affinities in Great Britain, they also came to hold an enduring influence within the U.S. church. The "gospel choir" later evolved into
prominence with massed choirs used around the world. From revival
hymns to gospel songs, African American concert spirituals, various
forms of gospel blues, and Pentecostal music, Christian music within
the U.S. church was inseparably linked with one's Christian faith
practices.

EURO-AMERICAN MUSIC IN DIASPORA

Since the time of the Protestant Reformation, Euro-American church music culture has defined itself through its hymns and accompanying worship practices. This was particularly true during the eighteenth and nineteenth centuries. Arising out of revival movements and generating new initiatives in mission, "hymn singing was a primary vehicle of the numinous, the very wind of the Spirit itself" (Marini 2006, 123–24). Only the Bible surpassed the hymnal as a definer of religious beliefs. Hymns accompanied Christian life at major church events and in daily living. Christian worship was intimately tied to the hymns and gospel songs of the day; songs functioned like folk songs where they were sung throughout society. However, the prevailing assumption was that to be a Christian, one automatically had to sing Western Christian songs. Thus hymns and gospel songs were inseparably linked with the Bible and Christian spirituality.

As waves of Euro-American missionaries left for Africa, they took with them the songs intimately tied to their Christian faith, completely unaware of how they would be received in new cultural settings. The close cultural affinities enjoyed between Europe and the Americas did not exist in the same ways between Euro-American cultures and those of Africa. In mission, the main goal was to preach the gospel, and for the most part, newly converted people learned to worship the way the missionary had worshiped in their home culture. The response to hymns and gospel songs in Africa, however, was not what early missionaries expected, and it was not what they intended.

FOR DISCUSSION

1. What is the history of music in your church? What are its origins? How does this influence your church's music today?

2. Identify four major reasons that missionaries introduced their own Christian hymns into the African church? Do you see similar approaches being done today? What are they?

3. "Let me write the hymns of a Church and I care not who writes the theology," declared the great Congregational preacher, R. W. Dale (Bradley 1997, 81). Based on this quote, discuss the implications for the use of music in the life of the church.

4. Identify five contemporary hymns that address current daily life struggles and contribute to a theology for the twenty-first century. Share with the class how they speak into your own spiritual growth and development.

5. CLASS PROJECT: Create a lyric theology portfolio of four churches in your community. Divide the class into four groups. Attend the same church service for four weeks in a row. Keep track of all the songs that are sung. Write out the full song text for each one, and identify the theological themes and scripture taught in them. Summarize by creating a lyric theology, that is, understandings and truths about God as found in the song texts. Then ask and discuss the following questions: if there were no sermons for four weeks of worship services, what would worshippers learn about God during that time through the songs? Is this sufficient?

3

Music Culture
African Life

Jean Ngoya Kidula

If you can talk, you can sing; if you can walk, you can dance
—Shona Proverb[1]

In 1902 Mrs. Saville and her husband, who were Church Missionary Society (CMS) missionaries, set up the first mission station among the Logooli of Western Kenya. In her report to the CMS mission in 1905, she wrote:

> In the morning we were at breakfast, a great din was heard outside, and a line of men in single file came prancing along, shouting at the top of their voices "Isa, Isa, Service akulanga . . ." (Jesus, Jesus calls us). Amidst the front of the house, they ran round and round in a circle and finally broke up amid yells of laughter, hugely delighted with themselves. It was hard to know whether to be amused or not for they treated it as a game, and there was something very pathetic in their singing such words which meant nothing to them. (Kasiera 1981, 187)

Ezekiel Kasiera records a musical encounter with this same group by a different missionary around the same time as the Saville report:

> At Kaimosi, Chilson [Arthur Chilson, a Quaker missionary circa 1905], attracted large crowds by a gramaphone that rendered such songs as '"All Hail the Power of Jesus Name." He noted ". . . they

came dancing and singing, blowing horns and making a great noise. Some were extravagantly decorated with ornaments, and red and white clay. Such a sight one will not see but in Africa. . . ." The nude Africans came from Idakho, Isukha and Tiriki with spears, bows and arrows to the beat of their drums.(Kasiera 1981, 180)

The African world in which North American and European missionaries brought the message of Christianity was viewed by each group through their musical cultural lenses. Although Mrs. Saville and her husband thought the performance of the Africans was pathetic, this unevangelized group's performance demonstrated their impression of what missionaries music sounded like to them because they were singing the song that had been taught to them by missionaries. Chilson, on the other hand, encountered a different response. In reaction to the gramophone, the culture group saw an opportunity for a music festival. As was the custom in this region, when "friendly" music was heard, different communities showcased their musical talent and styles, and in the process, exchanged ideas.

This chapter examines, through the eyes of explorers, missionaries, and colonizers and from the vantage point of what was documented of the African response, the African context that Euro-American Christianity entered. This two-sided coin recognizes

3.1 *Jula wedding dancers showcase their musical talent in contemporary Côte d'Ivoire.*

that missionaries brought understandings of Christianity rooted in their cultural interpretation of the Bible. Meanwhile, it presents the mindset of the missionaries of that time that all Africans were possibly the same, negating the many different histories, languages, and cultures of the continent. This chapter first describes how music was reportedly conceptualized in the worldview of those proselytized and ways that music established identity and articulated the beliefs, values, continuity, and change. Then the discussion turns to the implications for adopting a new religion and the possible impact and influence on indigenous cultures. Finally this chapter explores new types of music that are a result of contemporary global movements and how different missionizing agencies, African and non-African, embrace or reject these sounds.

Music and Cultural Life: Music for All of Life

Visitors to the continents were fascinated at how Africans incorporated music in their total life. Eileen Southern comments:

> [o]ne of the most striking features of African life was the importance given to music and dance, and travelers seldom failed to comment upon this. The earliest report in the English language comes from Richard Jobson, an English Sea captain sent to Africa by the Company of Adventurers of London in 1620 to explore the Gambia River area . . . 'There is without doubt, no people on earth more naturally affected to the sound of musicke than these people. . . . (1971, 6)

Oluadah Equiano, a former slave, wrote in his biography "We are almost without a doubt, a nation of dancers, musicians and poets . . . Thus every great event . . . is celebrated with public dances, which are accompanied with songs and dances suited to the occasion . . ." (quoted in Southern 1971, 6–7).

Portuguese explorer Duarte Lopes traveling in the Congo around 1591 remarked that "indigenous people celebrated feast by singing love ballades and playing flutes of curious fashion." He went on to describe the shapes of the flutes, the material from which they were made, the manner in which the instruments were played, and his impression of the types of sounds made on them (McCall 1998, 77).

In their encounters with Africans dating from the fifteenth century, missionaries, explorers, colonists, and other Westerners and

Northerners have remarked on the prevalence of music in the life of Africans. They comment on ideas about music, the multidimensional representations (aural, kinetic, dramatic, and visual), the performance, the involvement of the community, music's centrality in daily social, political, and religious life, and the diversity of musical instruments. Africa has fascinated its visitors by its holistic embrace of music in the fabric of it's people's lives. Such an approach seemed so different from the European one that, even today, there is an expectation that not only will Africans break into song and dance at the slightest provocation but that any person of African descent has an innate sense of "rhythm."

Observers perpetuated these stereotypical generalizations relative to practices in their own cultures. They were reinforced over time in books, journal, and newspaper articles or through reenactments in documentary and fiction films and videos. Scholarly disciplines, such as ethnomusicology, set up to study exotic and non-European music to justify these "differences" in a scientific manner, embraced the prevailing view of the time: that African music was "primitive" (Merriam 1964, 3–16; Wallaschek 1983, 15). John McCall sums up Richard Wallashek's appraisal of African music as shown in figure 3.2 (1998, 96).

Each of the components in figure 3.2 can be conceived positively or negatively, but at that time, they were intended to demonstrate the superiority of European music compared to any other in the world. Africans in the continent or in Diaspora voluntarily or forcefully justified or embraced these expectations particularly for survival. Texts were written by scholars to present the generalities of the different musics of Africa derived from case studies or as cumulative summaries reflecting prevalent scholarly thought.[2] Thus certain historical periods in the music of Africa have been frozen in contemporary practice, representing a static, rather than the dynamic, nature of the music and musicians of Africa on the continent and in Diaspora.

EUROPEAN MUSIC	AFRICAN MUSIC
modern	primitive
melodic	rhythmic
complex	simple
aesthetic	functional
mental	physical
intellectual	emotional
creative	expressive
product of culture	product of nature

3.2 European music compared with so-called primitive African music.

THE AFRICAN MUSIC WORLD

Faced with a continent of over eleven million square miles with more than three thousand ethnic groups, scholars of the music of Africa have traditionally subdivided the continent in two and used the Sahara Desert as the main demarcation. This subdivision was reinforced by prevailing ideologies on race and religion. Studies focused on sub-Saharan Africa. Most sub-Saharan Africans were darker skinned, not as Islamized as Northern Africans. They were considered by European enlightenment thought as primitive and by European Christianity as pagan. To better manage the study of the music in the cultural life of Africa, scholars adopted the culture areas concept posited by anthropologists and cultural geographers.[3] This concept classified African ethnic groups according to shared geographical, linguistic, and dominant cultural traits. Mainly applied for comparative purposes, this method proved useful in identifying the various instruments indigenous to certain areas of Africa, their variants, and dissemination to other parts of Africa and the world.[4] It also served to validate musical trends specific to cultures with particular social and political organizations. Consequently, certain principles emerged that have not only governed the study of the music of Africa but also suggested ways in which the most funda-mental definition—that is, the way of life of the people—governed the definition, theory, and practice of music. But more importantly, it suggested that social context was a prerequisite for understanding historical and contemporary African music. The most visible mani-festation of African music was musical instruments, and that was inevitably where most early scholars initially focused before moving to vocal music.

Music Instruments

The culture areas concept revealed that certain types of instruments dominated particular areas based on geographical features, environ-ment, and primary occupation. For example, there was a dominance of drums and drum ensembles in densely forested areas compared to those less forested because of the availability of wood to construct the body of the drum.[5] But more than geography was required to validate this statement. Relative to occupation, that is agricultural-ists versus pastoralists, and way of life, such as nomadic or not, some cultures living in forests had no drums, or the drums were borrowed

3.3 *African music instruments: top left, membranophones (Akan drums from Ghana); top right, lamellaphones (akongos from northeastern Uganda); lower left, chordophones (nzenze from northeastern Uganda); lower right, aerophone (chivoti from southern coast of Kenya).*

from their neighbors. This appeared to be true for the forest nomads of central Africa.[6]

The culture concept validated the preponderance of membranophones in West Africa, chordophones in Eastern Africa, lamellaphones in Southeastern Africa, and so on, but each of these was confirmed by sociocultural, political, and personal circumstances. Some instruments required elaborate ceremonials for construction by a few specialists (e.g., Atumpan drums of the Akan of Ghana), whereas others were created for personal entertainment (e.g., whistles by Nandi herdsmen of Kenya).

Instruments were played solo for self and group entertainment and education. For example, solo chordophones, such as the Zulu umqangala, which is used for self-expression and amusement, were also identity markers and educational tools in storytelling as characters or as accompaniment (Levine 2005, 59–61). Players of solo instruments could also be custodians of indigenous histories and values through song as demonstrated by Kora musicians of the

Manding' groups of the Sene-Gambia region. Solo instrumentalists therefore run the gamut of sophisticated professional technocrats to casual amateurs. Group ensembles ranged from instruments of the same type, such as Ewe drummers or Chopi xylophone players, to ensembles with different categories of instruments, such as those found among the Basoga of Uganda.

Instruments were considered only as musical artifacts in some cultures, whereas for others, certain instruments were symbolic of clan or political identity. As such, some instruments had clan or political totems inscribed onto their shape or body. The predominance of idiophones in the continent attracted a great deal of attention and not just for the sheer diversity of these instruments but also for the ways they were attached to the human body. These instruments somehow managed to turn the body into an instrument or melodic instruments became percussive through playing techniques or the addition of rattles to mask the timbre—for example, the addition of bottle-tops to the mbira of the Shona to create a buzz effect (Berliner 1981, 11–12). The migration of the instruments to other cultures fascinated organologists and comparative musicologists, providing conjecture or evidence for cultural and music history.

The Voice, Musical Structure, and Spectacle

Regardless of the culture area and whether or not it was accompanied by other instruments, vocal and choral music seemed to dominate the continent. Early descriptions of vocal music may have been difficult because of language barriers. Later scholars with better language facility state that vocal music was cultivated as group activity or for individual self-expression.[7] From choral and vocal music one learned the beliefs and values of the society, which helped the culture to survive, and they also learned musical aesthetics and artistry. It was also from studies of choral music that some of the generalizations of the characteristics of African music when compared to Eurogenic types were legitimized. These features included the practice of call-and-response as an organizational principle, the value of improvisation, metronome sense, the prominence of vocal vamps and claves, the idea of repetition as a structural element, the symbolic structures of text in metaphors or storylines, and the license music afforded text to address social, political, and economic mores and inequalities. Stylistic studies that compared types of African production against Asian or European vocalizations described the

3.4 Senufo Boloye: dance, drama, and spectacle in the Korhogo region of Côte d'Ivoire.

use of groans, moans, guttural sounds in emoting and as a preferred aesthetic. Thus vocal music included not just song texts but also performance practices.

Accounts of the different approaches to music by Africans comment on the integration of dance, drama, and spectacle with sound (Blacking 1967; McCall 1998; Nketia 1974).

Sometimes there was no need for sound because the spectacle invoked associations with specific rituals and therefore certain songs. For instance, when female circumcision was banned among the Kisii of Kenya, music, which was the main marker of the stages of the events and the transmitter of education for the female, was silenced. However the presence of the initiates in their regalia brought to the minds of those who had previously participated in the rite songs fundamental to that stage in the ritual.[8] Drama, dance, costume, and choreography were not just accompanying or accompanied by song but were integral in the structure of the music itself. Some of the materials used for costumes, such as raffia around the waist or a part of a mask, were integral idiophones that articulated the beat. Or they produced the percussive sound that was a preferred aesthetic in some cultures as fundamental to good music practice. The stamping of feet on wood or grass provided the rhythmic impetus for beginning phrases. The choreography of a circle not only reinforced cultural worldviews about the continuity of life, it also represented visual structuring of repetition as a musical organizational principle. Enacting ritual drama reinforced ideas and teaching from kinetic, visual, and physical senses. This layering of knowledge was such that it was not only heard, but also felt, seen, experienced, and expressed. Such an approach to knowledge acquisition enhanced the oral presentation and reinforcement of both individual and collective memory.

One of the earliest approaches of understanding the music of Africa was by studying its functions and uses in the cycle of life. In this approach, propagated by Alan Merriam (1964), a consolidated body of repertoire associated with a particular group assisted in the classification of genres. It identified them as lullabies, children's play songs, adult ritual songs, by gender and age group, genealogy and historical songs, story songs, and so on. The function and use of music in these multiple contexts was examined. This approach urged researchers to examine song or music beyond a particular function. For example, children's lullabies could contain text teaching the cul-

3.5 *Traditional dancers from Kampala, Uganda.*

ture's social hierarchy or relationships. The shape or anthropomorphic structure of an instrument could embody historical, social, political, or religious knowledge. Bodies of literature emerged that relegated most African music to function and use relative to activities and contexts, but they ignored professional music making for entertainment and self-expression. The most asked question in the study of African music became "What is it used for?" Composers and performers were subsumed into the community practice, and their individual contributions were largely unacknowledged. From this approach, some scholars analyzed the musical characteristics at different age levels and theorized on pedagogy and technical training at informal and formal gatherings, which facilitated a comfortable approach to public performance. Music was examined "essentially as a *social* activity," and musical structures were explored for their actual and symbolic representation of social hierarchies and relationships in society (Blacking 1967, 17, italics in original).

The Sacred and Secular in the Music of Africa

The obscure line dividing sacred and secular space has long intrigued observers of Africa. It may not mean the same thing as separating the holy and the profane because this delineation might be distinguished by scholars of African religion. Rather the invocation of the spiritual into the natural is evidenced in the practices and arts of daily life. For example, the central pole in the structure of a house of the Abaluyia people of Western Kenya symbolizes unseen powers and spirits in physical space. Although the pole itself has a practical architectural function, it also serves as a sacrificial altar or prayer pole—a daily reminder of the omnipresence of the supernatural in the natural.[9]

John Mbiti, a scholar on African religion states:

> Religion . . . is by far the richest part of the African heritage . . . is found in all areas of human life . . . has dominated the thinking of African peoples to such an extent that it has shaped their cultures, their social life, their political organization and economic activities. We can say, therefore, that religion is closely bound up with the traditional way of African life, while at the same time, this way of life has shaped religion. . . ." (1975, 10)

Thus religion was shaped by and shaped daily life. Music was, and is, a dominant part of both religion and daily life. For example, various readings could be applied when the same song is used at a funeral, a wrestling match, or a wedding.[10] The symbolism of such a song's versatility in multiple contexts is not lost on the listeners. The reincarnation of the song at various functions is expressed in the different formal and stylistic arrangement suitable for each performance space. In other cases, some instruments are played one way in one context and played differently in another. For example, sticks may be used in playing church drums and the same rhythms played with bare hands in entertainment venues (Kidula 2005, 220–21). This can be read to mean that the natural and the supernatural are intertwined and related. Music is also sourced from the metaphysical to the physical, or it is used to summon the spiritual to the material. Thus music is invoked in healing diseases or combating disasters, in that the spirits responsible for the malaise are summoned or dismissed through music (Friedson 1996 121–24, 163–69). One could also allege that musicians possess supernatural insights as a result of their ability to create the right atmosphere and context for negotiation with the unseen (Berliner 1981, 186–239). Therefore for some cultures, particular musics must be present to ensure communication with "the other."

THE IMPACT OF FOREIGN POLITICAL, SOCIAL, AND RELIGIOUS SYSTEMS ON AFRICAN MUSIC

New political and social systems and new spaces for performing indigenous music have changed the face and practice of African music. Some practices have been discontinued, whereas others have been reinforced. The urban area and migration has dispersed cultural musics beyond their initial geographical environment. South and Central African mine workers are well known for bringing the musics of their cultural groups into this new environment. The amalgamation of disparate nations into political states has also forced diverse musical practices to either freeze particular behaviors, clinging to them as authentic indigenous traditions, or to develop and expand forms and instruments as new ideas are incorporated. In other cases, new musics have been forged from these encounters, or some musics and instruments have been abandoned altogether (Askew 2002, 68–122). The formation of cultural troupes in many African countries at the dawn of independence attests to experiments in cultural continuity and amalgamation (Nketia 1986, 47–49).

It is impossible to summarize the music of such a vast continent in a few words. The prevailing worldview at the modern era's encounter with Africa assumed a uniformity of musical styles and instruments whose premises were rooted in the Enlightenment thinking of the time. In the encounter with European Christianity, African music almost always began in a position of unsuitability for worship because of its involvement with the African ways of life, which were deemed both pagan and uncivilized (McCall 1998, 75–88). These ideas contributed to the lumping of all African cultures together and the negation of positive ideas emerging from the continent. In the current age of globalization, African musicians highlight minute cultural differences, whereas generalizations and stereotypes are embraced by the larger world. This back-and-forth regarding the individuality of African cultures and the racializing of African peoples continues in political and economic encounters between the music of the continent and that of the larger world.

Makwaya

Makwaya is a well-known label applied to Christian choral music in Eastern Africa. Since the 1960s, makwaya music began to be accompanied by "secular" band music instruments associated with Congolese popular music customarily referred to as Soukous. They included a lead guitar, a rhythm guitar, a bass guitar, some percussion, maybe a drum and some brass instrument if the choir could afford them or if the sponsoring church was tolerant of the drums. The roles of the three main instruments were very similar to that of a dance band with the lead setting the pitch, the rhythm keeping time or articulating the style and the bass providing an ostinato groove that was at once melodic as it was harmonic. Musical conversations could be held between the lead singer and the lead guitar, or with the lead guitar and the bass, or even the lead guitar and the choir as was the case with a secular band. The text of the music was overtly Christian in theology or moral values relative to the denominations, and percussive instruments were generally avoided because of the tendency for people to dance in a 'secular' manner when they were present. Instead a 'Christian' style of stepping was adopted where the feet moved from right to left to articulate the main beats with little motion by other parts of the body that would suggest dance.

Music and Religious Worldview

The facet most contested by both Islam and Christianity in Africa relates to music in religion. (Here the broad definition of religion as a particular institutionalized or personal system of beliefs and practices related to the divine or interaction with deities is used.) Both Islam and Christianity considered African religions as pagan, and each of them sought to actively proselytize Africans. By the time modern Christianity encountered some African cultures, Islam already had a foothold, but not without intimidation tactics by the Muslims and resistance from many groups. In some cases, syncretism of Islam with African beliefs had taken such a strong root that African cultural markers, such as names, had already been replaced by Arab ones by the time European Christianity was introduced in the sixteenth century. For example, by the time new colonists arrived in the Senegambia in that century, "Islamic influence was stronger than Christianity," which had been introduced by Portuguese Catholics in the fifteenth century (Isichei 1995, 57). Music as a major force in religious and ritual practice was a contested site for political and social dominance by political and colonizing forces.

Depending on the brand of Christianity or Islam, new music was introduced, reinforced, or rejected with alternative storylines adopted. New poetic and musical forms and performance practices were required of the new converts. Certain instruments were associated with the different religious worldviews. African melody instruments and certain types of drums were prohibited from Christian worship, and instead, accordions, organs, or pianos were introduced when affordable.[11] At first missionaries initiated resistance to African instruments and the attitude was reinforced by some African converts. However, most singing was performed a cappella. Eventually drums and idiophones gained notoriety in congregational singing, but many African melody instruments still take a back seat to European and contemporary instruments in worship. Depending on Islamic denomination, singing in mosques is dictated by principles about the place and impact of music in worship.[12] However Asian instruments, such as the oud, dumbak, and harmonium, are heard at religious events, such as Mohammed's birthday. With the expansion of the media and global music industry, differences in sound and instrumentation between Christian and Islamic music are gradually blurring because composers, singers, instrumentalists, and audiences are exposed to similar sounds from around the world (see *Makwaya* and *Fuji* features in this chapter).

Music Makers and Audiences: Composers, Singers, and Instrumentalists

The distinction between music makers and their audiences has interested observers and scholars of Africa. Part of this intrigue was created by the types of performance spaces in which music occurs— frequently outdoors in a circle, partly to create an acoustic chamber, partly out of years of practice, and partly as an aesthetic preference. Creating a circle means that members of the performance group are visible to everybody, but each member can really be seen properly by the few that are close by, especially when there is a big group performing. This rather ambiguous placement ensures community and anonymity while promoting individuality and particularity. The audience is also often invoked to participate in the performance because the structure of the music requires them to clap on the main pulses or respond to the lead singer or instrumentalist. Many cultures made provisions for everybody to participate in music making in the ways they structured ensembles. For example, children's songs were performed by all, but to advance socially as a member of the group, these children might undergo an initiation ceremony that required members to perform certain musical acts. Thus communal music ensembles were demarcated by age group, gender, occupation, and even context.[13] These types of arenas provided training ground for future music specialists but also created a certain ambiguity to outsiders as to who was truly the best musician. Knowledge of the culture and participation in music activities taught members expectations for good or proper music.[14] It is also in such encounters and venues that new musics were tested, accepted, incorporated, or rejected by the culture. Thus one of the myths that every African can sing and dance has to be understood in the context of the intention of different groups with solo or ensemble opportunities for music making and validated by each cultures measure of what good or bad music entails, over against how music engenders group identity and solidarity.

Although there are few specialized instrumentalists in many cultures, many, if not most, people participate in choral music as singers. Many early scholars did not recognize the place of composers of these musics because the rules and understandings about copyright and ownership may have been different from those in Europe. The practice of improvization that encouraged individual creativity at each performance also devalued the importance of fixed compositions, instead encouraging the notion of a frame of reference, whether it was formal, contextual, individual, or durational to dictate the flow of the composition performance. With new approaches to rights legitimated by European colonialism and perpetuated by contemporary global social and economic markets, possession of music, texts, and innovations were redefined with individual ownership of compositions and arrangements superseding that of the community. This trend is particularly visible today in the academy and in popular music production.

Practices of the Christian church, particularly since the reformation and the Second Vatican Council, made music performance accessible to professional, amateur, and lay musicians. The church became the training ground for many musicians, particularly when this venue was the primary legitimate gathering place for the colonized and enslaved Africans. These arenas reinforced concepts posited as African—with blurred demarcations between audiences and performers, group participation, age, and gender and social classes as justified venues for learning not just appropriate music but the proper way of musicking.

Music and Modern Culture

The twentieth century forced a reworking of identity for most African groups. No longer did individuals identify themselves only according to their language or ethnic group; they were forced into countries subdivided by European colonial powers. One was no longer just an Ibo, but a Nigerian as well. Further, most Africans recognized themselves as Anglophone, Francophone, Lusophone, Arabized, and even had to align themselves with Christianity, Islam, or indigenous religions. Related to these constructs, social classes emerged relative to the adoption or rejection of mainstream national, linguistic, and even religious tenets. Each of these distinctions is now associated with the emergence and practice of certain ways of recognizing and doing music, including performance practices, styles of music, and sometimes, even different instruments. The impact of this alignment is felt in unprecedented ways.[15] Some instruments, such as the organ, were incorporated into religious repertoire, whereas many African instruments were discontinued.

New political leaders have an ambiguous reaction to this inclusion or exclusion of things African. On one hand, certain instruments, such as the guitar, are global and not just associated with one culture. But indiscriminate adoption of this instrument forces the country to give up some of its individuality in rejecting those instruments unique to their cultures. In the popular music realm, new musics emerged that were distinguished by region or country—for example, the association of *highlife* with West Africa and *kwela* with Southern Africa. These styles of music created new types of musicians, those that became proficient in European-type popular music instruments, singing about global topics, such as romantic love, but localizing social and political subject matter. But more than that, certain global music styles, such as reggae, rhythm and blues, and rap, have become staples in Africa, not just because they have strong African roots, but also because of what they represent for the urban and urbanizing population: a mélange of musical styles drawn from different quarters and global subject matter, such as romantic love or protest or social situations that are familiar sights in cities and towns across the world. These genres provide a way of voicing common human circumstances.

3.6 *The guitar alongside the nzenze and drum kit.*
Photo taken outside of Kasese, Uganda.

Christianity and Islam, on the other hand, have also birthed their own types of music especially recognized by timbral and structural elements. The preponderance of choir music in much of Christianized Africa attests to things as familiar as communal practice in indigenous societies. Some cultures recognizing different genres and styles by gender or age group. Choir performances also invoke the communal learning space as training ground for future musicians, with some instrumentalists receiving initial training in churches or church-run schools before venturing into the secular marketplace. Christian *makwaya* music is performed in a different vocal timbre and harmonization

> ## Fuji
>
> Fuji is also a well-known recreational style of music in Nigeria that originated from the Islamic community in that country. It assimilated praise song styles of the talking drum but avoided guitars—the hallmark of secular national popular music with distinctive Euro-American ethos. In the 1960s, the singers further invoked Islamicisms in their singing styles that were closer to wailing vocals and more strident than relaxed vocal techniques of Yoruba indigene. With time, Hawaiian guitar was invoked to accentuate the vocal style and synthesizers, trumpets, and other 'secular' band instruments appropriated together with the distinctive percussion arrangement that are hallmarks of the style.

than *taarabu* in Eastern Africa. Four-part choral harmony, strophic European poetic forms, and indigenous ethnic or semi-European tone color is invoked in *makwaya*, whereas unison singing, Swahili poetic structure, and nasalized Arabic tone is applied in *taarabu* music. In addition, it is rare that the oud is played to accompany singers in Christian or Christianized gatherings, but it will be used at Islamic or Islamized functions. Otherwise, standard contemporary popular instruments, such as guitar or keyboard, are common in both genres. In the past Christian singers dared not invoke an "Arab" aesthetic. However, the commercialization and nationalization of these two genres have promoted a marriage of musical ideologies rooted in what was originally posited as opposing cultures, the Orient and Europe. With the commercialization of religious music, gospel, *fuji*, and other contemporary religious genres are marketed as popular commodities. Modern cultural fusions blur the boundaries of secular and sacred, Islamized, Christianized, and indigenous genres.

MUSIC AND MEDIA: RADIO AND AUDIOVISUAL RECORDINGS

The dissemination of African music in contemporary society has been precipitated by the media, particularly radio, but also cassettes, compact discs (CDs), and video recordings. Of these, the radio has been the biggest and most effective tool for spreading African music styles and introducing the musics of other nations—African or not—to the continent. Although the radio was originally introduced in Africa to serve colonists, its impact greatly expanded during World War II as a means of reaching the public with news and propaganda (Stapleton and May 1987). Music punctuated or framed news, greetings, and other reports. Initial music types were either imitations of rumba, calypso, and other diasporic African genres or localized versions by emerging new musicians. Soon, African secular popular musics, religious Christian music, and eventually indigenous musics were aired. In time, popular secular and religious musics have come to dominate the airwaves, whereas recordings of indigenous performances have taken a back seat, displayed in most countries as educational pieces or circulated on ethnic-based shortwave stations. However, recordings of indigenous musics collected by scholars such as Hugh Tracey since the 1930s have become the impetus behind the "difference" in national and ethnic music and their variants in popular and academic, secular, and religious music practice.

There is no doubt that the media has hastened exposure to music of other cultures, countries, and nations. The media has also played a part in freezing traditions in structure and time. Music history attests that the development of new ideas occurred as a result of historical and cultural encounters. In Africa, however, a given sonic organization associated with an ethnic group, nation, or region is fixed such that musical, historical, and cultural innovations related to appropriation or acculturation of elements considered foreign, especially those associated with Wester European aesthetics, are usually not perceived as African. Much of Africa's musical innovations are often downplayed because dominant cultures tend to romanticize pagan and rural Africa—a notion rooted in the Enlightenment. In addition, much of Africa lacks adequate or sophisticated technology to showcase its citizens' inventions. It is only from the late 1990s that the contributions of individual musicians from Africa have gained international recognition. Dissemination was accelerated by such developments as access to the Internet in real time. Discussions in such forums and posting of musical materials have promoted the works of little known music cultures, artists, and innovations by African musicians—for good and for exploitation.

OBSERVATIONS

A Christian living or working in or with Africa is today faced with musical choices that nearly a hundred years ago were unimaginable. When European and North American missionaries with their respective home political systems sought to Christianize Africa, the definition of music in secular and religious lives may have been rather distinct, relative to their denominational and ethnic backgrounds. In many cases, African music was unsuitable. By the 1930s, some missionaries and proselytizers experimented with the use of African music composed in missionary styles, rooted in the Pentecostal spiritual songs, or adapted from the music of the groups they worked with. Meanwhile, European secular agenda and African political movements ushered in styles of popular and classical music considered appropriate for their causes. These musics were either performed as introduced or adapted and localized to either create variants or produce new songs. Nationalists since the 1960s have initiated cultural movements to reinvigorate, invent, and reinvent African musical arts. Meanwhile global encounters with contemporaries from other parts of the world were birthing new musics that became a part of the repertoire of musical resources available for the potential and actual Christian in Africa. As a result, a layer of music ideas and types are employed in Christian worship in Africa and by Africans. Different organizations often promote the types they think are most appropriate for worship. Because God cannot be contained by human limits, his creation cannot begin to understand or circumscribe the boundaries of the sounds that best speak of, or to, him.

FOR DISCUSSION

1. Identify the types and functions of music in African cultural life at the onset of the Euro-American missionary enterprise. How have the types and functions of music remained constant? How have they changed?

2. Identify the instrument types that were prevalent in different African culture areas. Have any non-African origin instruments been adopted? Why or why not? How have new instruments been incorporated in the styles and functions of music?

3. Do you or your culture, nation, or group subdivide and separate your daily undertakings into religious, secular, or profane? Why or why not? How does music function in your daily life and in that of your culture or situation?

4. Identify at least three types or styles of religious music that exist in your culture. Identify at least three types or styles of nonreligious music in your culture? Describe whether or not, why or why not, and in what ways if at all, the religious styles intersect with the nonreligious.

5. CLASS PROJECT: Design a chart or map of all the types or styles of music found within your culture, both religious and nonreligious. Show the distinctive characteristics and commonalities between the different musics. Indicate how the church has responded to each and incorporated these styles into the church.

4

Encounters
What Happens to Music when People Meet

James R. Krabill

Do not sing like someone else; do not dance like someone else.
—Cameroonian Proverb, *Mafa*[1]

For a long time already the Mission in Ivory Coast was waiting impatiently for May 30, 1922, the 25th anniversary of the ordination of its venerated Pastor, His Eminence Mgr. Moury. . . . The weather at day's beginning was magnificent. . . . Then the moment came and the procession, led by the cross and the choir boys, got underway to the joyous sound of bells. . . . Oh! What a perfect occasion for that song *Laetatus sum in his* which accompanied their march toward the church where the mystery of love of 25 years ago was to be renewed! . . . This marvelous day finally came to a close with 'The Hymn to Joan of Arc' (let's not forget that today is May 30) of which the refrain, sung by the entire assembly, was accompanied by the vibrant trumpets of the faithful brass band. (de S. G. Mgr. Moury and du T. R. P. Chabert 1922)

Africa's music, wrote Henry Weman nearly one-half century ago, is the mirror of the soul, "an essential part of [the African's] inmost being; it has the power to liberate, and it is in the music and the dance that the African can best be himself" (1960, 20). If Weman's statement is true for music in African society even before the arrival of Christianity, it should not be surprising then that music would likewise emerge as an important ingredient in the life and identity

57

of the newly formed Christian communities sprouting up across the continent. "*Ndiyanda kurinda!*"—"I want to sing!"—is, in fact, the way many Zambians announce their desire to take on the Christian faith—a faith, which for them, could only be adequately expressed in the outpouring of song (Sundkler 1980, 184).

For this reason, it is indeed unfortunate that many Western missionaries as Christianity's first messengers failed to tap traditional African music sources and open the door "whereby at least some of this wealth might pass across into the worship of the young churches" (Hastings 1976, 48). For some observers this constitutes a situation nothing short of "cultural genocide" and one of the saddest chapters and most regrettable aspects of the entire story of Western missionary efforts (Masa 1975, 157). All too common have been experiences similar to the one reported of an elderly man in Chad who confessed with hesitation to the local U.S. missionary, "I want to become a Christian, but . . . do I have to learn your music?" (Morse 1975, 35).

Chapter 2 detailed the various Western music traditions Euro-American missionaries brought with them to the African continent—Gregorian chant, hymns from the Protestant Reformation, Wesleyan and Victorian periods, gospel songs, camp meeting choruses, spirituals, and so on. Chapter 3 followed with a description of the rich world of music that already existed in sub-Saharan Africa, predating the arrival of the missionaries and continuing up to the present day. This chapter examines the encounter between these two music worlds more closely to see how they have interacted and together contributed to the African Christian music reality found in much of the church today. It looks at the encounter, first from the viewpoint of history and then from the perspective of religious change.

THE ENCOUNTER FROM THE VIEWPOINT OF HISTORY

The development of African Christian music has been a slow and arduous journey. According to Paul Willard Warnock in his important 1983 study, "Trends in African Church Music," this centuries-old story can be broken down into five distinguishable historical periods; he has identified them as prelude, foundations, consolidation, reassessment, and reorientation.

Prelude (1419–1736)

This period represents the first encounter of sub-Saharan Africa with European Christianity and begins with the coastal explorations of the Portuguese Prince Henry the Navigator. The earliest record of the Roman Catholic Mass being performed before African audiences was in 1482, first in Guinea and then again later that year in Ghana. Prospects for significant church expansion by Portuguese Catholics looked hopeful for a time, particularly in the kingdoms of Congo and Monomotapa and in Angola. But the close association of the mission with the commercial, military, and slave-trading interests of the Europeans was hardly conducive to communicating "good news." In one East African battle account from 1505, the Franciscan friars were first in line to step off their invading seafaring vessel and plant a cross under which they chanted *te deum laudamus* ("We praise you, O God"). At the completion of the song, "the place was given to plunder" (cited in Warnock 1983, 12–13). The encounter between Western missionaries and Africans during this period resulted in a largely unsuccessful endeavor to establish a lasting church presence in Africa.

Foundations (1737–1850)

For much of the latter seventeenth and early eighteenth centuries, European powers were preoccupied in places other than in Africa, thereby reducing missionary activity on the continent. But by the mid-eighteenth century, the first wave of Protestant missionaries began arriving from England, Holland, Germany, and elsewhere across Europe. These missionaries came in the spirit of their age, holding African music and culture in low esteem and bringing with them Western hymnody, which was destined to become the music of the new faith communities they were to found. One prevailing thought at this time, according to Katherine Morehouse (2006, 4–5), was that "different areas of the world were at various hierarchical stages of musical development and would eventually reach the level of excellence that Western music had already attained." Not surprisingly, it was precisely during this period, in Bruno Nettl's estimation, that the initial phase of "the most significant phenomenon in the global history of music," namely, "the intensive imposition of western music and musical thought upon the rest of the world" is seen.[2]

Consolidation (1851–1918)

What was laid as a foundation during the late eighteenth century was consolidated in the nineteenth century. This period represents what is generally referred to as the first phase of the Colonial Era in Africa—the carving up of the continent by the European powers at the Berlin Conference in 1884–1885 and the determined strategy on the part of all players to impose with increased rigor and force the "three Cs" (Christianity, commerce, and civilization), which were central to colonial policy, identity, and intentions. Mission schools and churches were seen by colonial administrators as useful instruments of the colony and were well placed to indoctrinate Africans in the religion, language, and culture of the colonizer. The Bible and the hymnbook had always been key tools in the hands of the

---

NTSIKANA
A MODEL FOR THOSE WHO WOULD PUT AFRICAN FAITH TO MUSIC

Ntsikana (c. 1780–1821) was one of the first converts to Christianity among the Xhosa-speaking people of southern Africa. Living at a time of growing conflict throughout the region, both among traditional chiefs as well as between the Xhosa and the encroaching white settlers, Nstikana served as a calming influence, a prophetic "servant of God," calling his people to prayer and peace and preparing the way for seeds of the Gospel to be planted and take root.

Some believe Ntsikana's first encounter with Christianity may have been as an older teenager when Dr. J. T. van der Kemp of the London Missionary Society lived for a year as an evangelist among the Xhosa in late 1799–early 1801. Though van der Kemp's efforts were short-lived and largely unsuccessful, it was perhaps here that Ntsikana first heard the Christian message.

Another important development in Ntsikana's spiritual pilgrimage took place fifteen years later when LMS missionary Rev. Joseph Williams opened a mission station in his area. Though Ntsikana never chose to settle at the station, he did visit Williams regularly for a few years, and while on the grounds, received some biblical instruction and participated in worship services held there.

Despite these occasional contacts, however, Ntsikana's exposure to Western missionaries was for the most part quite limited. Many Xhosa Christians, in fact, believe that Ntsikana's spiritual insights came directly from God with no assistance whatsoever from missionary agents. One such story, widely acclaimed and recounted, tells of a turning-point experience in Ntsikana's life when he reportedly saw a bright light strike his favorite ox, and later that same day, was prevented from participating in a neighbor's festive party when a whirlwind blew up out of nowhere, requiring the guests to abandon their dancing. Sensing that the Holy Spirit had entered him, Ntsikana ordered his family away from the dance, quickly took them home, and declared, "People should pray (rather than dance)!"

On the following day, Ntsikana exhibited strange behavior and could be overheard humming a melody unknown to his listeners. This was the beginning of Ntsikana's experience as an indigenous hymn composer. With time, he added words to the chant-like melodies he was receiving and expressed his faith in a set of four hymns, all of which were quickly taken over by the mission community and became part of the core of Xhosa Christianity.

In contrast to later Xhosa hymns, which were largely translations of English hymns based on European rhythms and melodies, Ntsikana's hymns were in the Xhosa language and made use of African idioms, rhythms, images and figures of speech.

One of Ntsikana's hymns is known as his "great hymn." In it, he praises *Ulo Tixo omkulu, ngosezulwini* ("The Great God, He is in the heavens"). He continues:

Thou art thou, Shield of truth.
Thou art thou, Stronghold of truth.
Thou art thou, Thicket of truth. . . .
Who created life (below) and created (life) above. . . .
The maker of the blind, does He not make them on purpose? . . .
As for His hunting, He hunteth for souls.
Who draweth together flocks opposed to each other. . . .
Thy blood, why is it streaming?
Thy blood, it was shed for us. . . .

missionary for teaching basic tenets of the faith; but during this era, some missionaries also valued hymns in particular for their capacity to initiate new converts into the Western musical tradition of hymn tunes and instrumentation being introduced to the worldwide church. This was clearly the tone of the observation made by Rev. W. R. Stevenson when he wrote with considerable excitement in 1892 (759): "The fact is that the best hymns of . . . English, [German and American] authors are now sung in China and South Africa, in Japan and Syria, among the peoples of India, and in the isles of the Pacific Ocean—indeed, in almost every place where Protestant missionaries have uplifted the gospel banner and gathered Christian Churches." It should be added that in reaction to the harsh colonial policies and the ongoing condemnation by many Western missions of "native initiatives" in church leadership and worship patterns, this period also witnessed the early signs of growing tension between church and mission in Africa and consequent interest among some African Christians in exploring indigenous church music as an African expression of the faith.

Reassessment (1919–1957)

In his massive study of French involvement in Central and West Africa, Jean Suret-Canale calls this period "The Zenith" or "Golden Age" of colonial history.[3] Having established a firm presence on the continent, the colonial powers used this period between the world wars to maximize their economic interests and extend their empires throughout the region and around the world. However World War II forced Europe to experience in a five-year period all of the tragedy that Africa had lived through during the previous sixty years. "Europe learned," wrote Ivorian novelist Bernard Dadié, "that the worst oppression of all was depriving people of free expression, preventing them from being themselves."[4] This change of attitude no doubt contributed to the softening of the church's attitude toward African music, which was bolstered, too, by increased scholarly research and new perspectives put forth at missionary conferences. A significant turning point for the Roman Catholic community came with Pope

4.1 *Catholic women of Porto Novo, Benin, transform royal praise song into liturgical praise.*

Pius XII's encyclical *Musicae Sacrae Disciplina* (1955) that encouraged missionaries to promote indigenous music in worship.

"Many of the peoples entrusted to the missionaries," it stated, "take surprising pleasure in rhythmic music and enhance the worship of their gods with religious music. It would not show much prudence on the parts of the heralds of Christ, the true God, if this effective means for promoting the apostolate be lightly thought of, or neglected" (Papal Encyclical 1955, 423). Such counsel "led to the production of the famous *Missa Luba* in Zaire and to the adoption of much new African music, especially in Rhodesia (now Zimbabwe) where the people regarded it as an expression of their resistance to settler rule."[5] A burst of musical energy was also found among the newly emerging African Initiated Churches (*AICs*), which were validated and strengthened by the surge of nationalism spreading across the continent. In Côte d'Ivoire, the Harrist Church and Papa Nouveau movement championed the rising resistance leader, Félix Houphouet-Boigny. They sang his praises in some of their hymns and compared him to a modern-day Moses, who was raised up by God to deliver them from the bondage of the French colonial regime (Krabill 1995, 270).

Reorientation (1958–1982)

The coming of independence to many African nations in or around 1960 opened the way to a new era in Africa, not only in the sociopolitical sphere but also in the life of the rapidly growing African churches. These years were characterized by the creative blending of Western and African musical traditions, an explosion of indigenous compositions in virtually all churches, and the incorporation of both contemporary, popular pan-African sounds and non-African musical cultures from the rest of the world into worship. Though Warnock's study ended in 1982, it would be accurate to say that many of the characteristics he identifies in the reorientation period would also apply to ongoing musical developments in Africa today. In addition to these traits, however, a more careful analysis of the post-1982 period would no doubt also need to highlight the increased use in many churches of "praise choruses," English and French-language song texts, American-inspired worship resources, and the almost universal adoption, from youthful, urban congregations to faith communities in outlying rural areas, of the drum kit and electronic equipment (i.e., sound systems, keyboards, and guitars). Though some might wish to refer to these recent developments as the globalization of African Christian music, more work needs to be done in identifying the cultural origins of these trends and the reasons for their appeal in the African context.

THE ENCOUNTER FROM THE VIEWPOINT OF RELIGIOUS CHANGE

A few of the historical milestones that have shaped the encounter between Euro-Americans and Africans in the coming of Christianity to sub-Saharan Africa have been examined. Now another encounter—the encounter between religious worldviews, most notably, Western Christianity and African traditional religion (or religions, in the plural, as many *francophone* academics prefer to call them)— needs to be considered. What can be said of this encounter that will help us to understand the development of African Christian music?

In 1900 there were an estimated ten million Christians in Africa, constituting about 9 percent of the total population. By the year 2000, just one century later, that figure had exploded to three hun-

---

THE MUSICAL LEGACY OF WILLIAM WADE HARRIS

In 1913, a fifty-three year old West African prophet-evangelist by the name of William Wade Harris left his native Liberia and stepped across the French colonial border into neighboring Côte d'Ivoire. He was equipped with little more than a passionate desire to share the good news of Jesus. Walking barefoot from village to village for hundreds of miles along the coast, Harris challenged people everywhere to lay aside their traditional objects of worship and turn instead to the one, true God.

Harris's ministry lasted a mere eighteen months before he was arrested by the French regime, beaten, and sent back to his native Liberia. During this brief period, however, an estimated 100,000 to 200,000 people from over a dozen different ethnic groups accepted the evangelist's call, received baptism, and took their first steps toward a new life in Christ. One of the questions frequently asked of Harris by new converts during their brief encounters with him concerned the type of music that they were expected to sing once they arrived back home in their villages. "Teach us the songs of heaven," they pleaded, "so that we can truly bring glory to God."

But Harris—though himself a lover of Western hymns learned since early childhood—refused easy answers. "I have never been to heaven," he wisely told them, "so I cannot tell you what kind of music is sung in God's royal village. But know this," he continued, "that God has no personal favorite songs. He hears all that we say in whatever language. It is sufficient for us to compose hymns of praise to him with our own music and in our own language for him to understand."

Encouraged by these words of counsel, new believers set to work immediately, transforming various traditional genres of music into praise songs to God. One such early hymn proclaims:

It was the Lord who first gave birth to us and placed us here.
How were we to know
That the Lord would give birth to us a second time?
Thanks to Him, we can live in peace on this earth!

In the years following Harris's swift passage throughout southern Côte d'Ivoire, and continuing right up to the present day, composers within the Harrist movement have written thousands of hymns, exploring new themes and developing additional musical styles as they learned to read the Scriptures and grew in Christian understanding. Some of these hymns tell Bible stories or relate events from Harrist history. Other texts function as prayers, mini-sermons, and confessions of faith—all set to music by members of the church, for the church, and in a language that the church can well understand.

dred sixty million, or nearly half of the continent's inhabitants. By any standard, this represents some rather significant religious change, So much so, that according to missiologist David A. Shank, Africa today holds the unrivaled distinction of being "the place where the largest number of people have moved into the Christian stream of history in the shortest amount of time."[6]

It is neither helpful nor accurate to think of African Christians and their churches as some kind of generic, monolithic grouping

4.2 William Wade Harris with his followers.

of like-minded people. In fact, in a 1984 survey, some seven thousand distinct indigenous movements were identified as existing in forty-three countries throughout the continent. Altogether these movements claimed seventy-one thousand places of worship and a total membership approaching twenty-eight million, with more than eight hundred thousand new members joining each year. Since then, the numbers have only increased. In the 2001 edition of the *World Christian Encyclopedia*, African Christians identified as "Independents" were reported at eighty-three million and "Pentecostals/ Charismatics" at one hundred twenty-six million. Of the members classified in these two groups, 65 percent were found in three countries: Nigeria, Congo and South Africa.[7]

Perhaps even more important than the geographical scattering and sheer numbers of these movements, however, is the cultural, religious, and theological diversity found among these groups. In part, this is as a result that many, if not most, of them are entirely local and indigenously African in polity, program, leadership, and finance. Also significant is the fact that each of these movements finds itself at a different place on a continuum in the encounter between traditional African beliefs and practices and the Western version of Christianity to which many of them were initially introduced.

Harold W. Turner was one of the first scholars to observe a spectrum of identifiable reactions to this encounter.[8] He began with those groups only a step removed from traditional African reli-

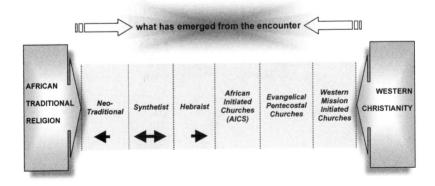

4.3 *The Encounter of Two Belief Systems.*

gious reality and spanning the gamut to communities most clearly modeled after and connected to the Western mission agencies that gave them birth (see figure 4.3).

Neo-traditional groups result from Africa's encounter with Western Christianity but are generally shaped and affected by the encounter in relatively minor ways. Western influences may manifest themselves in the use of certain "powerful" words (e.g., Alleluia), gestures (e.g., the sign of the cross), objects (e.g., a photo of Pope John Paul II on the altar), or vestments (e.g., high church robes or headgear). But these movements are far more interested in reinvigorating the enfeebled and threatened traditional religion than in adopting the "white man's" foreign and imported faith (see direction of arrow). Their music is entirely homegrown and rooted deeply in the languages, music systems, and imagery of the local context. The Niankan movement in Côte d'Ivoire with its self-proclaimed "black prophet-messiah" was in the 1970s to 1990s characteristic of such groups.

The terms *synthetist* and *hebraist* are Turner expressions. Synthetists groups refer to movements that are intentionally drinking from both Western Christian and African religious streams and making a creative, unique synthesis of the two (see arrows). Albert de Surgy's important work on Celestial Christianity in Benin is a helpful window into such a movement (2001a). Hebraist groups, although grounded firmly in African soil, are more deliberately moving away from certain aspects of traditional religion (see arrow). They are adamantly anti-fetish and emphatically monotheistic with considerable focus on "worship of the one true God." Their emphasis on God's law (the Ten Commandments and aspects of the Levitical and purity codes), sacerdotal leadership, worship space as "holy ground," and their lack of christological focus and clarity gives these movements an Old Testament, hebraist feel and character. The Déhima movement in Côte d'Ivoire, with its warnings to all would-be worshipers to discard and forever leave behind all their fetishes in a rubbish pile at the church door entrance before entering God's house for worship, might be offered as an example of this kind of group. Synthetist and hebraist movements, like the neo-traditional groups before them, compose their own music for worship and make little if any use of songs from Western music sources.

AICs, referred to in earlier days as African *Independent* Churches, are also tied closely to African traditional styles and structures, but they tend to represent more Christ-centered, spirit-led, biblically oriented expressions of New Testament faith. These are the first of these groups that I have called churches. The former groups, in Turner's analysis, are generally referred to as new religious movements. *AICs* are deeply committed to being Christian in thought and practice but see little need to become Western to do so. Many AIC Christians and their leaders were one-time members of Western mission churches but eventually chose to part ways or were expelled for precisely this reason. Because of historical connections to Western missions, some *AICs* have taken with them the hymnals of parent mission churches or in some other way incorporated Africanized versions of Euro-American music into their worship.[9] However, composing new African-inspired chants and songs is also placed in high esteem among many of these churches. Examples of *AICs* in Africa today include some of the Zionist churches in southern Africa and certain groups within the white-robed "praying," or *aladura*, churches (e.g., Church of the Lord and Cherubim and Seraphim), originating in Nigeria and now firmly implanted in virtually every nation across West Africa.

The so-called *Evangelical Pentecostal* churches have, for the most part, only recently been added to the scene in the African religious mix of things. When Turner did his 1960s research in various locations across West Africa, they were virtually nonexistent as a

4.4 A spiritual church in Ghana sings and dances unto the Lord.

phenomenon to contend with. Albert de Surgy's important work on these churches in Benin illustrates just how quickly they have sprouted up throughout the region (2001b, 11). From only 9 registered churches in 1955, denominations grew in Benin to 36 in 1980, 81 in 1986, 96 in 1994, and 163 at the end of 1997. Many, though not all, of these churches were of the Evangelical Pentecostal variety. Paul Gifford's work (1993) on these churches in Nigeria, Ghana, and Liberia and Allan Anderson's effort (2001) to situate them within the "global charismatic family" of churches is helping to create a profile of their worship, life, and activities. Though it is still too early to draw many conclusions, a few of the characteristics beginning to emerge include classic manifestations of spiritual gifts (e.g., speaking in tongues, prophesy, and such), a Bible-centered faith, considerable evangelistic zeal, and an energetic style of worship; these are characteristics in many, not all, of these churches. They have a tendency to think of themselves as less "syncretistic" than the AICs and more "spiritual" than the Western mission initiated churches (WMICs). Growth is particularly evident for these churches in urban settings where young adults, migrating from rural areas, find them upbeat, cosmopolitan, and meeting their needs. Sunday attire, leadership patterns, worship format, and musical styles are often quite Western. But the inspiration for this is less the local WMICs than the radio and television evangelists, the international globetrotting inspirational speakers, and the freely circulating audio or video cassettes, and digital video discs (DVDs) of ministers and musicians from locations across Africa and throughout the Western world.

Despite the rapid growth of the Evangelical Pentecostals, the WMICs (e.g., Roman Catholic, Lutheran, Presbyterian, Reformed, Anglican, Baptist, Methodist, North American independent/non-denominational, and so on) still make up by far the majority of the Christian population in sub-Saharan Africa. Their story has intersected in most cases with the history of the European colonial empire described in a previous section of this chapter. These churches are the longest standing and most visible vestige of the encounter between Western Christianity and the precolonical religious traditions of Africa. Many such churches have gone through various stages from "imported" hymns to culturally rooted or locally produced compositions over decades or even centuries of music refinement and development. And the hybrid of worship music they are creating today is for many of them in an exciting but perpetual state of experimentation and change. Over twenty years ago, I was invited to attend a grandiose Sunday morning worship service bringing together more than a thousand members of the Western District of Côte d'Ivoire's Methodist Church. Six choirs and one brass band performed a total of thirty-seven hymns throughout the course of the nearly three-hour celebration. Of those hymns, no less than thirty-five were of the Western imported variety—twenty-seven of these (including Handel's "Hallelujah Chorus") being furthermore reproduced in the French language, with the remaining eight (including "Joy to the World") translated into local languages. Only two of the songs performed qualified as indigenous compositions. But all that is changing quite rapidly for many WMICs as newer, often more dynamic AICs and Evangelical Pentecostal churches raise the musical bar and as these churches themselves begin to delve more deeply into the rich cultural heritage that is theirs as African people. Some such churches are already well down the road in this direction, and others are only now beginning the journey.

Six Stages of Music Development in Many African Faith Communities

Some churches and religious movements in Africa have from the beginning sung their own locally composed music. In certain instances, such as the Harrist movement of Côte d'Ivoire, the use of imported music has not only been discouraged but also forbidden for nearly a century (see feature, "The Musical Legacy of William Wade Harris").

However, many if not most other churches—particularly those of the Western mission initiated variety—have passed, or are currently passing, through a number of stages on their way to developing a music for worship they can call their own. Identifying a few of these stages will help to explain yet another level of the Western-African encounter that has taken place since the chanting of that first Latin Mass on the west coast of Africa in 1482.

The six stages are: importation, adaptation, alteration, imitation, indigenization, and internationalization. I do not mean to imply that all churches have passed through every one of these stages or have done so in this precise order. The stages occur frequently enough however to be helpful in the reflection on what happens to music when people meet.

Stage 1: Importation

In the importation stage, hymn tunes, texts, and rhythms all originate with the Western missionary. For much of Africa's church history, the hymns of Isaac Watts and Charles Wesley, portions of the Latin mass, or "The Hymn to Joan of Arc" were simply taken over from the West and reproduced as accurately as possible by new believers in African worship contexts. Interestingly, over time, many African Christians came to genuinely cherish Euro-American music traditions and consider them as their own. Asante Darkwa (1980), speaking for many other Ghanaian Christians, has noted that "the hymn tune is perhaps the most commonly understood form of Western music by literates and preliterate Africans. Christians sing their favorite hymns not only at church services but also at wakes and burials and in other situations in which they find solace and comfort in those ancient and modern hymns which have done a wealth of good spiritually to Christians all over the world" (69). Catherine Gray reports a similar situation among the Baganda in Uganda where Western hymnody "is now so much a part of Christian worship and Baganda life that it could be called indigenous music" (cited in Morehouse 2006, 10).

4.5 A Mennonite choir in Ghana.

Not all Africans, however, have felt as "at home" with Western musical traditions as this might suggest. There has persisted with many people a deep lingering and underlying sense of alienation, of "spiritual unsuitability," in the Western music legacy introduced by the missionaries. Nigerian E. Bolaji Idowu stated it most harshly forty years ago when he wrote (1965, 30–31): "Again and again, as we have observed, choirs have been made to sing or screech out complicated anthems in English while they barely or do not at all appreciate what they are singing. . . . We must not be deceived by the fact that people have borne their martyrdom to this infliction without complaint so far."

Stage 2: Adaptation

In the adaptation stage, imported hymn tunes or texts are in some way "Africanized" by rendering them more suitable or intelligible to worshipers in a given setting. Nothing is substantially changed with the imported hymn tune or text at this stage of development. But an effort might be made to adapt the tune to the context of a particular faith community by introducing the use of drums, rattles, or other locally produced instruments. The Cherubim and Seraphim Church frequently does this with well-known Western hymns, as illustrated

4.6 Incorporating local instruments into worship.

by their version of "What a Friend We Have in Jesus," accompanied by harmonica, drums, and cow bells (Krabill 2006). Or the decision might be made to translate the text of a hymn from a Western language into a locally spoken one so it can be better understood. There is no attempt or desire here to change the actual text of the song but simply to render it accessible in another language.

Translating hymn texts has been a common practice throughout much of the missionary era and is generally as helpful to new converts as it is satisfying to the missionaries themselves. "You cannot appreciate what it means to hear 'Nothing but the Blood of Jesus' sung in a strange language away out in a bush town!" reported Christian and Missionary Alliance workers in 1930, one year after their arrival in Côte d'Ivoire.[10] It must be noted here, however, that translated hymns—though perhaps more fully understood than those remaining in a "foreign" language—are often little more than "short-cuts," "temporary stop-gaps," and in any case "from the point of view of their art, not the best" (Nketia 1958, 274). One common predicament is that many African words, based on tonal patterns, have their tones and meanings altered when they are sung to Euro-American tunes. One serious case is reported by Idowu when the English expression "miserable offender," translated into Yoruba and sung to a certain European tune, became "miserable one afflicted with tuberculosis of the glands" (1965, 33).

Stage 3: Alteration

In the alteration stage, some part of the missionary's hymn (tune, text, or rhythm) is replaced or otherwise significantly modified by an indigenous form. What happens at this stage is more than a simple translation of Western tunes (with rattles) or texts (with language) into an African idiom, it is rather a substantial alteration or total substitution of some part of the Western hymn by tunes, texts, or rhythms of indigenous composition or flavor. Examples of this type of modification might be: (a) hymns in which Western tunes are retained but new, locally written texts replace the Western ones;[11] or (b) hymns in which Western texts are retained and put to new, locally composed tunes. Vatican II's *Constitution on Liturgy* ("Sacrosanctum Concilium," no. 38) has allowed for variations and adaptations of the liturgy along these lines and has engendered a lively debate in African Catholic circles about the need for "cultural enrootedness of the liturgy" and "incarnational Eucharistic celebrations" (Krabill 1995, 42, n. 58).

Stage 4: Imitation

In the imitation stage, tunes, texts, and rhythms are locally composed or performed but in a style that is inspired or replicates in some way a Western musical genre. According to Asante Darkwa (1980, 69), "nearly all the well-known Ghanaian composers, as well as students, have tried to write hymn tunes." One of the most famous of these was Dr. Ephraim Amu, who as an expert in Ghanaian traditional music, studied at the Royal School of Music in London (1937–1940), and who eventually composed and published a collection of forty-five choral works (Amu 1993). More recently, Gray has reported from Uganda on songs warning about the dangers of AIDS composed in "hymnodic stanzaic structure" (cited in Morehouse 2006, 10). Illustrations abound from elsewhere across the continent where African musicians have composed songs for worship in the styles of nineteenth-century revivalist hymns, southern gospel, four-part male quartet arrangements, and increasingly on the contemporary music scene in the popular genres of "praise and worship" choruses, country and western, hip-hop, reggae, and rap.

Stage 5: Indigenization

In the indigenization stage, tunes, texts, and rhythms are locally produced in indigenous musical forms and styles. Many first-generation Christians in Africa have resisted using indigenous tunes, languages, and instruments in worship because of the emotional and spiritual associations these tend to conger up of their former lives. The church and its "music makers and managers" (see chap. 6) need to take this matter seriously and avoid any unnecessary temptations or "stumbling blocks" for new believers. What is also true, however, is that nothing more inspires and brings to life the church in Africa than singing and dancing the indigenous "heart music" of the culture. Whenever such music is introduced into the African worship experience, something almost magical immediately sets in. "At once," writes Idowu (1965), "every face lights up; there is an unmistakable feeling as of thirsty desert travelers who reach an oasis. Anyone watching . . . will know immediately that [the] worshipers are at home, singing heart and soul" (34). Indigenous, locally composed music does not need to be the only diet for the church. But a healthy church will make it a goal. For "when a people develops its own hymns with both vernacular words and music, it is good

4.7 Singing heart and soul in the Democratic Republic of the Congo.

evidence that Christianity has truly taken root" (Chenoweth and Bee 1968, 212).

Stage 6: Internationalization

In the internationalization stage, tunes, texts, and rhythms from the global faith family beyond the West and one's own local context become incorporated into the life and worship of the church. This is the newest, almost unexplored, frontier of worship music for the church. In contrast to contextual music, it is what the 1996 "Nairobi Statement on Worship and Culture" has called "cross-cultural" music.[12] This will be "the" encounter of the twenty-first century, vastly broader and richer than the bilateral relationships that have characterized so much of the colonial experience between Europe and Africa up until now. The internationalization of music encounters holds great promise for the church because it moves us ever closer to that ultimate encounter described in Revelation 7:9-10 when all languages, tribes, and nations will together proclaim, "Salvation belongs to our God, who is seated on the throne, and to the Lamb!"

Moving Forward: Respecting the Past and Creating the Future

In the years to come, African Christian music will almost certainly be characterized by an increased surge of dynamism and creativity as inherited music traditions from the past find their way into the blended worship of the future. For in the end, writes Warnock, Africans have never allowed themselves to be dominated by Westerners.

> Once committed to the way of life proposed by the missionary, Africans made the necessary adjustments to increase the enjoyment they could derive from the new music. They made conscious and unconscious adjustments of tunes and rhythms. They allowed hymns which they disliked to drop out of circulation. They started their own churches where they hoped to enjoy the benefits of Christianity without the unwanted trappings. In subtle ways the African was showing that he was in control of his destiny. The history of African church music is fascinating not so much from the standpoint of what the missionaries did, but how the Africans responded to the missionary impetus. Even when severe restrictions on musical expression were in operation, African Christians were able to filter the music through the African personality and create something new. (1983, 275–76)

Professor B. Makhathini of the University of Swaziland proposes a fascinating image to describe how the African church is working to creatively deal with the legacy of Western Christianity as it moves from the past into the future. For him, Western Christians took the "bread of life" (the Christian faith) they had received over the centuries and put it in a plastic bag (their own customs). When they arrived in Africa, they fed people the bag along with the bread. "Now, the plastic bag is making us sick!" says Makhathini. "The plastic is theirs. We know that God planned for us to receive the bread just as he planned for them to receive it. We can remove the plastic, and enjoy the bread."[13]

Enjoying the bread without the plastic—that is apparently what increasing numbers of Africans are doing as the continent moves each year further down the pathway to surpassing all other continents as the largest heartland of the Christian faith. And as it does, a new kind of reverse cross-cultural encounter will almost certainly occur that no one could have ever imagined just a few short years ago.

4.8 New musical encounters in Benin.

I caught a glimpse of that encounter recently when I attended an evening concert given by a Congolese church choir on tour in the United States. About forty-five minutes into the presentation, it was announced that the choir would be teaching the mostly white and slightly stiff middle-class audience a "sing-along song."

With a twinkle in his eye, the director turned to the crowd and said, "Now I know that for many of you, the music you've been hearing tonight likely has some strange harmonic patterns and a bit more rhythm and movement than you are used to. But let me tell you a secret. When we get to heaven, all of God's children are going to gather together and take a vote on what kind of music we're going to sing. Now you've probably heard about the incredible growth of the church in the global South. Well, guess who's going to win the vote? (The audience breaks out in hearty laughter.) So, if there's a chance you might be singing this kind of music *forever*, don't you think it would be a great idea to get started learning some of it right here *tonight?*"

CONCLUSION

The encounter between Western Christianity and Africa's tradi-tional religion(s) has produced a wide spectrum of vibrant responses throughout the sub-Saharan region of Africa. In all of the churches or movements that have emerged as a result of this encounter, music has played, and continues to play, a vital role. When one stops to consider the sheer volume of musical production being generated across the thousands of movements and denominations and the tens of thousands of local worshiping communities in Africa today, it simply boggles the mind beyond comprehension.

The dynamic encounter between African and Western music traditions will no doubt continue unabated in the years ahead. And perhaps the life and counsel of Ghana's hymn composer and ethno-musicologist, Amu, is the best we can do in imagining how the two will coexist as separate yet hybrid realities. As a young student and professor during the peak of the colonial era of the 1930s and 1940s, Amu consciously chose to free himself from the cultural expecta-tions of his day by refusing to dress in Western-style clothing and wearing traditional Ghanaian cloth made out of locally spun cotton instead. Yet Amu clearly lived biculturally with great ease in both Western and African worlds and reportedly loved to serve soup to guests in earthen pots and water in calabashes on a table adorned with imported cutlery. "There is no harm in embracing the *good* things of other cultures that have *universal* values," Amu once said, "but by all means let us keep the best in our own."[14]

FOR DISCUSSION

1. What are the primary cultural and historical forces that have shaped the formation of Christian music in Africa today?

2. Do you agree with Chenoweth and Bee that "when a people develops its own hymns . . . it is good evidence that Christianity has truly taken root"? What are the implications of this statement for churches in the North American cultural context?

3. What lessons can be learned from the ministry of William Wade Harris? How did his approach to hymn creation compare with or contrast to prevailing colonial attitudes at the time? Do you think his approach would still work today?

4. Can you name the six stages of musical development discussed in this chapter? How would you describe the differences between them? Should one of these stages be an "ideal" for the church in Africa today?

5. CLASS PROJECT: Review the section of this chapter that describes what happens to hymns in the alteration phase of musical development. Then try some alterations of your own by either: (a) taking a well-known secular or religious song text and putting it to a different tune, possibly one of your own composition or (b) choosing a popular, recognizable tune and writing your own accompanying lyrics. Once this exercise is completed, discuss as a group if, and how, these alterations have changed the feeling or meaning of the song in its original form.

5

Church Music in the Life of African Christian Communities

Thomas Oduro

To sing the song of the elephant is to go along the path cleared
by the elephant.
—Ghanian Proverb, *Akan*[1]

DIARY OF A CHRISTIAN FUNERAL—A LONG EXPRESSION OF GRIEF THROUGH MUSIC

After returning to the USA from Kenya for the summer, I was trying to get back into the rhythm of student life before the 1993 fall classes when I got an unexpected phone call. My father, whom I had seen barely 4 days before was dead, probably of a heart attack. Of course, I did not believe it. He had not been sick when I left. I did not accept this news until I got to the mortuary in Kisumu town where Dad had been taken while the family waited for me to get home and to the village. It was unheard of that a burial was delayed while waiting for an unmarried daughter to come home. I was setting a precedent, but so had my grandfather and my father when they became Christians.

At that time, a death in the village was announced by wailing. As people gathered at the home of the bereaved, the arrival of any new mourner was greeted with wailing and then singing around the body of the deceased. If the deceased was a Christian, Christian hymns, songs and choruses were sung before each new mourner was led into the house and given a cup of tea and maybe some food. But each time a new person arrived, a group of people ran to meet them. Sometimes, the new arrivals announced their coming with wailing in which case,

81

they were joined by others on the road and around the compound in wailing, and then led to the body where there was singing and prayers. This pattern continued until the funeral service 2–3 days later.

Since my father had been taken to the mortuary, there was much wailing, but not much singing, until his body was brought home. Then the action began. My father's body was driven to the church and then to his home, accompanied by singing and dancing. The music was a combination of celebration, grief, comfort, catharsis etc. After my father was laid out in the covered balcony, any new arrival was greeted with wailing and singing. By 7 o'clock, these sounds had become part of the environment. At around 8:00 p.m. my sisters and I gathered in front of my oldest brother's house and sang my father's favorite songs in English, Swahili, Logooli, and any other language, from children's songs, to church songs, to folk songs. We also sang our favorite songs.

My brothers were too shocked by the suddenness of the death to join in. An hour later, we heard the sound of traditional sukuti rhythms (Sukuti is a song, dance, drum type) in the distance. My cousin, (a lead sukuti drummer) who was not a Christian, had gathered his friends to come and mourn his uncle. Everyone perked up while we continued to sing for a while but it was evident that there was going to be an interesting confrontation between "tradition" and "Christianity." Usually these kinds of music were not accepted at funeral sites of known deceased Christians. My father was not only a Christian; he had been the General Secretary of a Christian denomination for years. My cousin's troupe arrived on the outskirts of my father's compound and their sound permeated surroundings to the extent that people joined in the singing. He did not enter the compound as he knew the controversy that would arise from the church elders if he came in.

But his pain and statement was heard and a response was generated by the "Christian" groups that had been eating and chilling in the compound. They picked up the church drums and began to sing in contest against the group outside. They sang spirit songs, choirs from different churches performed special numbers or took over a portion of the evening to lead in song, women's groups led the singing, not just around the body, but around the house and walked through the village celebrating not so much the life of my father, for the songs were not about him. They were Christian songs; some already incorporated in the culture as part of funeral rites, and others just goodtime songs, spiritual songs. The songs and the drama kept the crowd awake all night. By 6 in the morning, everyone dispersed to prepare for the funeral. The only sounds now were wailing and singing around the body when a new mourner arrived. This behavior continued until 10 a.m. when the funeral commenced.

*The funeral service had speeches, eulogies and a sermon, inter-
spersed with hymns, "spirit" songs, and special numbers by different
groups including churches, schools and organizations that had come to
honor my father. Because of the threat of rain, the burial service was
conducted much faster than usual. It had a singing processional led by
a group of women wearing white dresses in double file. They walked
behind the pallbearers, the family singing missionary and indigenous
hymns in a funeral processional style. After some prayers, the body
was lowered into the grave and covered with soil, all this accompanied
with singing. After the grave was completely covered, my mother and
the family were led into the house to the singing of the group. Usually
this is a leisurely walk but because of the rain, it was a much more
brisk escort. After more songs and prayer, the mourners sat down in
groups to share in a meal.[2]*

HISTORICAL REVIEW OF CHRISTIAN COMMUNITIES IN AFRICA

The story of Christianity in Africa is composed of multiple encounters. The first encounter, from roughly AD 62 to 1500, was the time
Christianity flourished in North Africa and Ethiopia. The second
encounter, from 1400 to 1800, was the period of Portuguese navi-
gational evangelism, and the third encounter, from 1792 to 1918,
can be said to be the Protestant missionary era. Europeans and Africans who were converted to Christianity by Europeans championed these encounters (Baur 1998, 21–152). One can easily denote
fourth and fifth encounters: the period of AICs[3] and the period of
the Charismatic/Pentecostal churches. In this chapter, the history of
Christianity in Africa, south of the Sahara (excluding Ethiopia), is
reviewed in regard to the efforts of the Roman Catholics and that of
the Protestants before outlining the creative musical developments
with the African church.

Roman Catholic

News about the conquest of Constantinople by Muslims in 1453
and the turning of Christian worship centers into mosques in the
then-Christian world made the Portuguese vow to attack Muslims
and reclaim Christian lands. Expeditions under the supervision of
Prince Henry the Navigator, son of King João I, who was ably given
papal support, found success in introducing Christianity to Africa.
Although the Portuguese had many motives for circumnavigating
Africa outside of Europe (Sanneh 1983, 51–52), Pope Nicholas'

permission to the Portuguese king in 1452 to "reduce Muslims, pagans and other enemies of Christ to perpetual servitude" leaves no doubt about the missionary motives of the Portuguese (Baur 1998, 47). The conversion of a Mandingo chief in Gambia to Christianity in 1458, the establishment of Christianity in Gold Coast (now Ghana) in 1471, the building of chapels in trade Castles, the training of local chaplains, and the subsequent Christianization of the kingdoms of Kongo, Angola, Matamba, Warri, and other city-states in East Africa were all pioneering efforts of Roman Catholics to evangelize Africa and, thus, establish Christian communities (Baur 1998, 43–98).

The pioneering efforts of the Catholics were full of challenges. Some of the Portuguese traders were more concerned about making profits at the expense of proclaiming the gospel; the lives of some of the priests were in contrast to the gospel they preached. Most of the Africans they attempted to convert were also more interested in trading than changing their faith from African traditional religions to a white man's religion. The trade in slaves destabilized the work of the missionaries; it put a big question mark on the genuineness of the freedom the missionaries were proclaiming. Despite all these challenges, the Catholics laid a solid foundation for future Western missionaries.

Protestants

Three strands of Protestantism have been introduced to Africa. They are WMICs, AICs, and Charismatic/Pentecostal churches. I will discuss each of the strands briefly.

Western Mission Initiated Churches

One of the major efforts by Protestants to establish Christianity in Africa was inadvertently caused by the transatlantic slave trade. The discovery of the "new" world, that is, the West Indies and America, in 1492 brought to the fore the need for more slaves to work in the mines and plantations. This need heightened the transatlantic slave trade that was also called the triangle trade. Slaves were bought in West Africa and shipped under inhuman conditions to the new world. The products from the mines and agricultural plantations were in turn shipped to feed European factories. The trade in slaves blossomed in Europe and the new world despite its inhuman practices.

5.1 Presbyterian Church of East Africa: Bahati Martyrs in Nairobi, Kenya.

A series of revivals in Europe (the Pietists, the Moravians, and the Evangelical revival in Great Britain in the eighteenth century) and the Great Awakenings in the Americas set the pace for missionary activities in Africa. Protestant Christians became conscious of the need to live godly lives and spread the gospel to other lands. Many mission agencies and societies for the promotion of Christian literature were formed during this time. The slave trade was, consequently, abolished. The mission agents sent many missionaries to Africa, then known as the "Dark Continent," to evangelize it. Educational institutions and medical centers, among other facilities, were established to entrench Western civilization in Africa. All this led to the spread of Protestantism in Africa. African Christians, as a result, were grouped into communities known as Presbyterians, Methodists, Anglicans, Baptists, Salvation Army, Seventh-Day Adventists, and many others.

African Initiated Churches

From the eighteenth to the nineteenth century, Christianity in Africa was not different from Christianity in Europe and America. The liturgy, architecture, education, worldview, and ways of proclaiming the gospel were all done either exactly or with little modification

> ### THESE POOR NATIVE PAGANS
>
> "These poor native pagans had to be clothed in Western clothes so that they could speak to the white man's God, the only God, who was obviously unable to recognize them unless they were decently clad. These poor creatures must be made to sing the white man's hymns hopelessly badly translated, they had to worship in the white man's unemotional and individualistic way, they had to think and speak of God and all the wonderful Gospel truths in the white man's well proven terms."
>
> —Desmond Tutu
> (Fasholé-Luke et al. 1978, 365)

from that of the West. Christianity in Africa was, consequently, called the "White Man's religion." The process of evangelizing and Christianizing Africa was fraught with many challenges for Western missionaries—Catholics and Protestants alike. Prominent among those challenges was overcoming the deeply entrenched traditional religions in the lives of Africans, learning the various languages, and integrating African cultures and worldview into Christianity. Many Western missionaries accepted the challenge of studying African languages and reducing them into written languages. The immense role of the traditional religion in African societies was greatly minimized. The greatest challenge was how to integrate African culture and worldview into Christianity in a way that would make Christianity more meaningful and relevant to the Africans. That challenge was enormous because of the many strands of African culture and worldview that stood in sharp contrast to Western civilization.

Some Africans began to acknowledge the dichotomy between Western philosophy and civilization and African worldview and culture in their respective Christian communities. Of particular interest to the Africans was the denial of the reality of the existence of demons and other malevolent spirits by Western missionaries in Africa, the need for empirical means of protection from such spirits, the use of spiritual gifts, such as healing, the employing of prophecy to enhance the growth of the church, the integration of African forms of liturgy in Christianity, and the extrication of all forms of Western domination over the African Church. These issues made the realization of integrating African culture and worldview within Christianity a sheer impossibility. Some Western missionaries and their African agents resisted the call to make such radical changes in Christianity before the eighteenth century. Matters, however, got

5.2 Africa Israel Ninevah Church with flag in Nairobi, Kenya.

out of hand in the nineteenth century; this led to the emergence of a new Christian community called variously African Independent/ Instituted/Initiated/Indigenous Churches. The AICs are Christian communities that have been able to integrate African culture, customs, and worldview to Christianity. Their form of Christianity is more culturally connected to the pre-Christian religious experience of Africans.

Charismatic/Pentecostal Churches

The Charismatic/Pentecostal Christian community are Christians who believe in the baptism of, or with, the Spirit, deliverance from evil spirits, the use of spiritual gifts, such as prophecy, healing, and the centrality of the Holy Spirit in church life and polity. The outpouring of the spirit on members of the church in Jerusalem some weeks after the ascension of Jesus Christ has been traced to the beginning of Charismatic/Pentecostal Christian communities (Acts 2:1-13). Modern Pentecostalism is traced to the revival on Azusa Street in Los Angeles in 1906 (Hollenweger 1977, 22). Even though Pentecostalism in Africa is widely believed to be established through the ministry of Johannes Buchler, a former Baptist pastor who planted the Christian Catholic Church in Zion in South Africa in 1895 (Anderson 2001, 94–95), there are several instances of people who spoke in tongues in Africa without hearing about the ministry of Buchler (Larbi 2001, 63–67). The establishment of Charismatic/ Pentecostal Christian communities in Africa has, therefore, been through the efforts of both Western missionaries and some Africans who do not have any historical links with Western missionaries.

THE MUSICAL HERITAGE OF WESTERN MISSIONARY CHURCHES

Music played important roles in the worship styles of Western missionary churches that were planted in Africa. Different kinds of music were introduced to Christian communities of Africa. Some of them were composed and sung many years before the establishment of the church in Africa.

> Among the most loved of all medieval hymns was one dedicated to the Virgin Mary, *Stabat Mater Dolorosa* (The Mother stands in sorrow), and a Passiontide hymn, *Pange lingua* (Sing my tongue), by Venantius Fortunatus, who also wrote *Vexilla Regis* (The Royal Banners Go). Theodulf of Orleans . . . wrote *Gloria, laus et honor* (All Glory, laud, and honor) which remains the principle Palm Sunday hymn for most of Western Christendom to this day. Another favorite was the solemn dirge of a thirteenth-century Franciscan, *Dies Irae* (Day of Wrath). (Volz 1997, 155)

The Mass was celebrated with hymns and songs composed by Western musicians and used since the medieval period. The songs were sometimes sung in the Latin language. Antiphonal songs featured prominently in the celebration of the Mass. Protestant churches in Africa made elaborate use of music in their worship settings. The use of hymns, anthems, and canticles became a regular feature during worship. Methodism in Africa, in particular, is characterized with the singing of hymns. Churches, which were planted in Africa as a result of revivalism in the United States and Europe, introduced Western choruses and some Negro spirituals. Many African Christians, however, often did not understand some of the lyrics of the hymns. "What can an African villager make of hymns to the Trinity that use language like 'consubtantial, co-eternal, while unending ages run'?" (Pobee and Ositelu 1998, 42).

Using music in worship was not introduced to Africans by Western missionaries and the churches they planted. Before the planting of the church in Africa, Africans were using music prominently in their traditional worship. The songs that were sung by Africans were, however, not documented; they were passed on from one generation to another or from one worship community to another. The songs were, therefore, not sung on a wider scale; they were limited to certain worship communities. The lack of documentation of the songs caused the loss of many of them. This was as a result of death, migration, and the gradual lack of interest in certain ones.

Songs brought to Africa by Western missionaries were by contrast documented and distributed widely. The life span of songs was, as a result, ensured. Because congregations of Western mission-founded churches were planted across tribal boundaries, the singing of hymns and songs tended to forge unity among tribes. Some of the hymns were beloved and sung by many people. As a result, though independent in many respects, the singing of Western hymns is a prominent part in many AICs in South Africa as stated by Paul Makhubu:

> In church, hymn singing is a major part of worship. The preacher becomes more inspired by singing. If the singing is dull, the service and preaching become dull. At funerals, hymns express deep sorrow. They are sung sincerely and with meaning. A moment later another hymn may be sung expressing joy of being a Christian and going home to heaven, another hymn expressing some part of Christian life may be sung. (1988, 71, 72)

One other heritage with hymn singing is memorization. Although Western hymns are documented, many Africans could not use them because they were illiterate, and the practice of looking into a songbook to sing was strange to Africans. The solution to these two discomforts was found in the art of memorization. Makhubu states this vividly:

> Blacks are good memorizers; they know almost all the hymns by heart. No matter how many verses there are, they know them all. There are very few books at Zionists services. Hymns are not announced, or where to find them in the book. One starts the hymns and different voices join naturally. This memorization started with the church founders when many of them could not read or write. (1988, 72)

When the Western missionaries introduced hymn singing to Africans, little did they know that Africans would sing hymns

5.3 Singing hymns from a book in the Democratic Republic of the Congo.

differently than was practiced in their Western congregations. Africans, on the other hand, did not know that hymn singing would sharpen their skills of memorization.

Before the introduction of Christianity, communal group singing was the norm in most African worshiping communities when they met to worship. However, the introduction of the worship choir was a new phenomenon in the worship life of many African communities; selecting a group of worshipers to sing vocally in four-part voices from a book has been one of the heritages of Western music in Africa. The concept of a church choir is so beloved by most Africans that they uncritically wear the choir robes that the Westerners introduced, even though the robes are not conducive to the warm weather of the users. Church choirs in the Democratic Republic of Congo, formerly Zaire, serve as a case in point.

> The popularity of Church Choirs in Africa is, for example, seen in the hesitation of the Marxist government of Zaire (now the Democratic Republic of Congo) to ban choirs alongside all youth groups that were perceived to be rivals of the Union of Socialist Youth, a youth wing of the government. . . .

The choir was the focus of the Congolese congregation. It dominated the lives of participants. Rehearsals required participation three evenings in a week, followed by the final manifestation on Sunday in the chapel, and accompanied by accordion, guitar, drums and diverse other rhythmic instruments. (Sundkler and Steed 2000, 963)

The theology of Western hymns has become a veritable teaching tool for some African Christians who do not have the privilege of attending Bible colleges and seminaries. Many African Christians use the hymns and songs as means of ensuring spiritual growth. Western hymns and songs are accordingly used in prayer and meditation.

African Christians Create and Transmit Their Faith in Song

New ways of composing church songs have arisen; the days when African Christian communities sang only songs composed by Westerners are few. Africans now compose their own songs for worship. It is interesting to note that there are different kinds of composers. There are those who have studied the dynamics of composition at music schools that are patterned on Western musicology, and there

5.4 Women's choir in the Democratic Republic of the Congo.

> ### SINGING COMES NATURALLY
>
> "Singing comes naturally. In other words, every black person is a natural singer. If anyone starts singing, others follow naturally and fall into harmonic parts naturally. Blacks love singing at all times. At work, when lifting anything heavy, it is done with song. When digging trenches, rhythm regulates the raising and falling of the pick. Singing permeates the life of a black person."
>
> —Makhubu 1998, 71

are composers who have no formal knowledge in the art of composition. The latter group claims to "catch" their songs through dreams, visions, and other esoteric experiences. The gift of catching songs is prevalent among many Christian communities in Africa. The phrase is, however, widely used by members of The Church of Jesus Christ on Earth through the Prophet Simon Kimbangu, an AIC also known as the Kimbanguists.

In composing songs, they do not leave out their peculiar theologies and worldviews. Therefore, songs about the reality of the devil and demons are common in many African churches. Protection from malevolent spirits has also become a common feature of African Christian hymnodies. Vernacularization of African hymnodies and gospel songs has been a great agent in transmitting their faith. These days Africans sing gospel songs with meaning. The lyrics are in their vernacular so they understand every bit of the songs they sing. They also express their deep feelings in a meaningful manner. The literate and the illiterate, alike, now sing without any hesitation. Local rhythms have been woven into local choruses in most African Christian communities. The rhythms naturally evoke local dances and choreographies. The discussion now turns to how African Christian communities use music in certain settings.

Worship

Music plays prominent roles in Christian communities in Africa. When Africans meet to worship they sing their hearts out. In fact, music takes about three-quarters of the duration of worship in many Christian communities in Africa. It is the worship setting that portrays the musical ingenuity of Africans. The whole congregation sings local choruses and Western hymns. When the entire congregation sings local gospel choruses they break into various harmonic tones, usually more than the traditional four harmonies—soprano, alto, tenor, and bass. The harmonies come naturally and are sweet scented.

Group singing is another aspect of worship style among Christian communities in Africa. The groups are varied and at times are gender based, peer based, or mixed. Church choirs are not left out during worship. They sing both Western and local choruses and anthems. At certain times the singing is left to soloists who sing only the melody. Worship settings, particularly, among AICs are lively. Makhubu describes the worship

> ### AS THE DANCERS TAKE HOLD
>
> "As the dancers take hold of a Catholic feast such as Corpus Christi, they incorporate it into their dance, their own history, as well as celebrate the kingship of Jesus Christ. The successful execution of the dancers' delicate steps, and other body language, become a dramatic and ritually expressive way in which Jesus Christ is reconfigured and honored."
>
> —Olupona 2000, 395

of an AIC in South Africa thus, "The music is loud and the singers sing loudly, screaming, jumping up and down on stage, sweat running down their bodies. They let themselves go. The audience screams. Drums and vocal singing are dominant over the instruments" (1998, 33). The use of locally made music sung in local rhythms with local instruments has enlivened worship in many African Christian communities. The immense growth of the church in Africa cannot be mentioned without this fact.

5.5 Pressure drum from Burkina Faso.

Choreography and drum language have been the latest inclusion in the worship setting of many African Christian communities. At such worship settings, the attributes (appellations) of the triune God are first played on the drums and interpreted simultaneously by someone who is skilled in interpreting drum language. Jacob Olupona describes the various dances of the Asantes and how Catholics in Kumasi, Ghana, use some of the dances to praise God (2000, 379–86). Thus the triune God is not only praised verbally, he is also praised with music, dance, and drama.

Evangelism

The role of music in the proclamation of the gospel is another phenomenal creativity in African Christianity. Evangelism in many parts of Africa is done on the streets, at market places, at hospitals, in prisons, and on buses and trains. Radio and television are other means of evangelism in many African countries. Many evangelists use music both as an attention getter and a message enforcer. It is common to see the audience joining in singing with the special songs that precede the evangelistic messages. Through music, people gather willingly to pay attention to the evangelist, and at times, the songs reinforce the subject matter of the message.

Celebration of Life Cycles

Life cycles in human beings are events that are celebrated elaborately in many African communities:

> Life is characterized by movement; the child, who may be regarded as a passive member of society moves from that stage into puberty or young adulthood, where the initiation rites performed usher him into adulthood. Then comes marriage, procreation, old age and finally death, which ushers the person into the land of the spirits. (Opoku 1978, 103)

In most African Christian communities, celebrations include birth, baptism, puberty rites, confirmation, marriage, and death. Ensuring that the transition from one life cycle to another is smooth is usually the main motive of the celebration of the events. Christian communities and families of both spouses celebrate them. Music, once again, plays an important role during such occasions. Songs that suit the occasion are selected and sung. People sing and express their feelings openly. Performing the rites is also done alongside the singing of songs. The use of music during funerals, as stated at the beginning of this chapter, stresses the essential role of music during ritual performances of life cycles.

MUSICAL DEVELOPMENTS IN THE CHURCH IN AFRICA TODAY

The church in Africa continues to use songs in creative ways; ways other than that of the period when Western missionaries were in direct supervision of African Churches. The discussion now focuses on some of these new ways of using songs in the church.

Spontaneous Hymnodical Hermeneutics

Among some Christian communities in Africa, particularly the AICs and the Pentecostals, the arts of homiletics (preaching) and hermeneutics (interpretation of scripture) are done by the entire congregation. During worship services one person is designated to preach a sermon. He or she prepares the sermon without consulting any member of the congregation, but during the preaching of the sermon other members contribute to the theme of the sermon. How is that done? One example comes from the Kimbanguists church:

> After the opening hymns the preaching begins, but members are free to interrupt with songs of their own choosing at any point.

5.6 *A group of Baptist believers set scripture to song in Côte d'Ivoire.*

> They are particularly likely to jump in and lead off with a song whenever the preacher hands over to a reader. . . . It is sometimes difficult for the preacher to regain control of the service unless the chanting dies out naturally. These songs are nevertheless regarded by the preachers as a valuable reinforcement of their message and the success of the meeting depends on the degree to which the members have experienced *possession* by the Holy Spirit. (Dickson 1992, 180)

The songs, at times, explain the message or give deeper interpretation to the theme. One person may interrupt the sermon with a song that denotes either a parable or a teaching of Jesus Christ concerning the theme of the sermon.

Apart from using music to aid preachers in delivering their sermons and interpret the Bible well, there is another way of using music to show appreciation to lead preachers. Among Harrist churches in the Côte d'Ivoire, members of a congregation assemble at the home of the head preacher to lead a procession from his house to the church. A recession is similarly made from the place of worship to the home of the lead preacher. Both the procession and recession are marked with joyous singing and the playing of bead-enmeshed gourds ("calabashes"). The worshipers use this means to express appreciation to the lead preacher for accepting his call and ministering to them through prayer, the written word, and preaching.

The Catholic Mass

The liturgical reforms by the Second Vatican Council in 1962 have led to many innovative ways of celebrating the Mass and other events in the Catholic Church. An example can be cited from the Archdiocese of Kumasi in Ghana. "The Asante Diocese under Bishop Sarpong has . . . composed and employs liturgical songs based on local tunes and idioms; and makes use of local musical instruments such as drums, flutes, shakers, and xylophones" (Olupona 2000, 375). The creative role of music in the celebration of the Mass and other Catholic festivities has given a new understanding of the sacrament, thus enhancing participatory ownership.

Using indigenous musical instruments and dances are not limited to Catholics. It is becoming more common for Christian communities in Africa to use musical instruments that are homemade in their respective ethnic environments to worship God. Local

5.7 This local drum kit was played in a Baptist church near Kasese, Uganda.

instruments that are used to worship God differ from one community to another, even in one denomination. Combined together with the use of local musical instruments are local rhythms and dances. As a result, liturgical diversity has become the norm among various Christian communities in Africa.

School Choirs and Workplace Choirs

Another phenomenon in some parts of Africa is the forming of school choirs and, more recently, workplace choirs. Members of these choirs may not necessarily be Christians or belong to one denomination. These choirs are made up of people who have an interest in singing and who come together during free periods in educational institutions to learn songs. In the case of workplace choirs, they meet during lunch break. The choirs sing at functions organized by their institutions and are sometimes invited to sing at state functions. Workplace choirs are usually sponsored by their parent institutions. School and workplace choirs tend to unite Christians and non-Christians alike.

5.8 Evangelicals recording newly composed scripture songs in Bouaké, Côte d'Ivoire.

Preservation of Church Music: Recording Local Hymns and Songs

A greater number of the songs sung by Christian communities in Africa are not preserved in the traditional Western way, that is, through staff notation. By contrast, songs are recorded either on a cassette or a compact disc (CD). Recorded gospel songs are played on radio and television stations, at homes, beer bars, restaurants, and in automobiles. There is a commercial advantage of this method of preserving gospel songs. Those engaged in playing the musical instruments, recording, mixing, packaging, wholesale distribution, and retailing all find themselves in profitable job opportunities. The recorded songs are sung on a wider level than those preserved through staff notation because the latter method needs one who can read the notes before teaching. The recorded songs need no specialist to teach; one learns them by singing along.

Music as Pedagogical Tool

One of the various ways Africans make use of music is the narration of Bible stories in music. Composers skillfully put into music some of the beloved stories in the Bible. Such songs usually end with moral applications and lessons. This means of singing was used as a form of pedagogy as a result of the low rate of literacy in Africa. The majority of such songs are antiphonal, based on a call-and-response form. They make lasting imprints on the minds of both singers and listeners.

CONCLUSION

This chapter has traced the historical incorporation of various Christian communities into the lives of Africans and their concomitant musical practices, including the Western, mission-based musical heritage and African-inspired Christian music. It also identified the various ways African Christians use music in addition to those introduced by Western missions and missionaries.

Africans are known to be genetically musical. They hardly do anything without the embellishment of music. The African funeral scene at the beginning of the chapter clearly epitomizes the use and role of music in the lives of Africans. In times of political upheavals, civil wars, persecutions, death, unemployment, loss of jobs, sickness, and any kind of predicament, African Christians use music to inspire hope and to press on with equanimity. The more they listen to or sing songs, the more they are comforted and assured of God's omnipotence and goodness. Music plays a vital role in building the faith of many African Christians and also facilitates utter dependence on God. Christianity has, therefore, been received and practiced with music.

FOR DISCUSSION

1. "Music plays a great role in the growth of the church in Africa." How true is this assertion? Discuss the many ways in which music has played a role in the African Church and its growth.

2. Music has been an integral part of death, funerals, and burials in many ethnic groups around the world. Describe what the atmosphere would be at a funeral and burial service in which there is no singing or music.

3. "The claim of *catching songs* through dreams, visions and other esoteric experiences is undoubtedly against the norms of accepted musicology and must, therefore, be rejected by all trained musicians." Discuss.

4. CLASS PROJECT: AICs are churches or Christian communities that have been able to integrate African culture, customs, and worldview into Christianity. Divide the class into three groups and locate an AIC, if possible. If there is not an AIC in your area, locate an African church that practices a more African style or non-Western style of worship that differs from your own church. Each group must locate and worship with an AIC. Each group must present a report on the role of music in an AIC worship service. If possible, each group should make an appointment with and interview the leader of the church regarding music in the church.

6

Making and Managing Music in African Christian Life

Jean Ngoya Kidula

Those who love music do not mind carrying drums on their heads.
—Ghanian Proverb, *Akan*[1]

His voice rose from the back row, clear, loud, and strong. He was singing an easily learned piece but in a language none of us recognized. He eventually made his way to the front of the church. The pastor excitedly welcomed him into the church through prayer, interjected by traditional collective words of encouragement by the congregation. We thought we recognized that voice, but we were not sure. We dared not open our eyes before the end of the prayer, but we were anxious to confirm our conjectures. After we said our collective 'Amen' and opened our eyes, we saw him; the village thief. He was the one with the new song—a spiritual song. What on earth would this mean to the village and to his family's heritage? That was a matter to be negotiated. Acceptability did not only have to do with broader cultural issues regarding the singer's position in society, it was also the music. Was the style acceptable in church? Was the music itself or lyrics trustworthy given what everybody knew about the composer? Was there a wait period to ensure that the performer was serious about his faith to accept the song into the musical canon? And who legitimized the person, style, and durability of the song?

Music is invariably an identity and culture marker. It is made and managed by its practitioners in composition, performance, and installation as tradition. Not only do the sights, sounds, and movements distinguish music of a particular group, time, or space, but certain

101

individuals also inevitably become custodians of the process and product. Culture groups and historical eras have developed unique ways to acknowledge these custodians as initiators, performers, critics, or consumers. In today's world, live and canned performances are avenues and venues for venerating or rejecting music creation, management, and consumption. It is also in these arenas that traditions and their carriers are reinforced, negotiated, or changed.[2]

CHRISTIANITY AND MUSIC IN AFRICAN LIFE

The introduction of European Christianity into African life with its accompanying music led not only to the acquisition of new styles of music, but also to entirely different ways of making and managing music.[3] New notions of music ownership came into play even as it was recognized that the music was intended for community consumption, used for evangelism, prayer and praise, teaching and training, personal devotion, and as an alternative to indigenous song. This functional approach to music and the idea that all African music was pagan satisfied only these particular dimensions of the impact of

---

IN HER AUTOBIOGRAPHY

In her autobiography "Twenty years in Africa 1913–1933," Mrs. Marion Keller, a missionary of the Pentecostal Assemblies of Canada, recounts how and why she introduced European instruments and hymns to young converts:

> . . . I organized a rhythm band. I selected thirty little girls and boys not over twelve years who were in the second grade in school, and gave them such instruments to play as did not require the knowledge of notes, such as cymbals, drums, castanets, bells, triangles, tambourines, and blocks. It has been a huge success and it is remarkable how very well they do in keeping time. I get a thrill teaching them and they all enjoy it very much. Now it is not so difficult to keep their voices together in singing as it was before. I lead with the piano while the big bass drum and cymbals start with me, followed by the smaller instruments in rhythm time. . . . Please pray . . . for the African youth. They have greater temptations than you realize. If we take all their enjoyments away from them, the heathen dances, and various worldly pleasures when we present the Gospel to them, we must give them something that will take their place. They do love all kinds of music, and sing the songs of Zion with great fervor and vim. The Gospel hymns can be heard resounding through the air, especially in the evening, these take the place of heathen dances . . . (Keller n.d., 57–58)

music and provided no repertoire for non-Christian social activities. Thus Christian music and European or North American folk songs, styles, and ways of approaching music became the norm rather than the alternative. But equally disconcerting was the struggle to be African and Christian. Although it was almost clear what being a Christian entailed in terms of new rites and rituals, these establishments did not respect African identity markers, such as names, social relationships, occupations, and the like.[4] The expectations of the colonial government politically and economically undermined cohesive cultural life, forcing groups to migrate, mingle, and reconfigure relationships among themselves and in relation to the new imposed political systems. The negative effect of this deliberate and unreasoned attitude toward identity continues to plague the representation of Africa and its music on the world stage. Meanwhile the introduction of European Christian music provided new creative resources.

Given the diversity of African cultures and their multifarious musics and the missionary zeal to earn converts to particular Christian persuasions, some musical approaches that worked well in one culture or with one denomination were not necessarily suitable in another. As a result, many different kinds and styles of European or North American musics were introduced, sometimes to the same people, depending on the assortment of missions in a given language group or culture area. These varieties were invoked for 'secular' contexts as the need arose due to prohibitions on the use of indigenous African music.

ENCULTURATION AND CONTINUITY OF MUSIC IN AFRICAN CHRISTIAN LIFE

It was clear from the onset that the first types of musics learned were from the missionizing agencies' own backgrounds, whether they were chants, hymns, gospel songs, or other musics (Nketia 1974, 13–17). Although these songs and hymns were translated into African languages to be employed as in the original European or American culture or denomination, it was equally clear that as Africans were anglicized or assimilated into French culture they attached similar or different functions or meanings to the musics introduced to them as Christian. Although translation of hymns was the primary avenue for introducing new repertoire, some denominations accepted spiritual songs, and others sought to adopt Christian words to African tunes wholesale or with alterations to style or performance practice.[5] Musical responses to changes in theology or social or political systems in Europe and the Americas were taken to the field as well. For example, with shifts in musical styles, instruments, such as guitars, became part of the religious endeavors particularly from the late 1950s onward. With the charismatic explosions of the late 1960s, the praise and worship repertoire of African and non-Africa sources are vital elements in Christian gatherings. Since the beginning of the encounter between African believers and missionaries, the believers have, independently, or in affiliation with missionaries, developed their own theological understandings and accompanying musics. The Christian industrial revolution that gathered global momentum from the end of the 1970s brought new dimensions to the role and place of the music production and consumption in religious circles. It is this diversity of musics and musical behavior that missionaries and church leaders still beg to either understand or manage.

Along with the introduction of new repertoire in the musical history of the church in Africa have been new ways of making and managing music (e.g., Corbitt 1994; Ekueme 1971; Jones 1976; Kidula 2000). In European or Eurocentric culture, individual composers and arrangers are venerated as originators and owners

6.1 *Daystar University students in the Christian ministry training music course in Nairobi, Kenya, play drum and guitar side by side.*

of songs, with regulations to manage the dissemination and adoption of the product by others. This trend was evinced in church as most hymnals normally include the name of the composers of the text and tune. The contemporary music industry has extended individual ownership through copyright rules and regulations, whereas academic institutions, many of which were first set up by missionaries, recognize ownership through notation and transcription.

Music Ownership and Management

The practice of individual ownership has not been extensively practiced in African music cultures. Instead, group participation and individual appropriation tends to be the norm. Although individual composers and performers have been recognized, many African language groups, states, and nations favored communal ownership of music or distinctive performance practices as identity markers.[6] The resilience of a musical piece or way of doing music established the said repertoire and technique into the accepted canon of dynamic traditions. The dominance of Eurocentric political and economic ideology and the amalgamation of disparate culture groups into nation-states led to layered approaches to production, consumption, and ownership. Some pieces of music were acknowledged as collective culture-group or national heritage, whereas other repertoire ascribed to dominant Eurocentric global ideology, with the individual composer or performer as the recognized originator. Music in Christian circles has been treated in the same way with hymns, choruses, and some spiritual songs considered public domain regardless of international copyright rules. Other music, like gospel songs, arranged spirituals or newly composed repertoire, guided by Eurocentric models, whether emanating from an Afrogenic or Euro-American source, identify and acknowledge the perceived originator.

Aside from economic and political factors, making and managing music in the African church has been influenced by exposure to global theological and musical trends. Different generations adopt types of music accepted as Christian—such as the veneration of hymns or gospel songs by the generation introduced to Christianity by hymn-singing Euro-Americans. Older people have been slower to accept global secular trends, unless they have been acceptably incorporated in the musicscape, than the current generations who are exposed to global trends available on the market or in the media. In cultures or contexts with only recent contact with Christianity, two musical approaches can be identified and several others can be derived from these two. In one case, as in the first modern encounters of European Christianity with Africa, evangelizers introduce the music they are familiar with. This music may have an African or other source. Thus Kenyan missionaries in Ethiopia or Sudan or U.S. missionaries in Cameroon or Congo will introduce the types of music they are familiar with from their home bases. In another case, missionaries seek to encourage new converts to compose or use music because it is culturally appropriate or structured by the new believer's world. Thus missionaries in Somalia might encourage storytelling songs as a way to reinforce Christian teaching or ideas, and those in Côte d'Ivoire might invite the culture's musicians to compose appropriate Christian songs in styles or structures that are familiar and acceptable to indigenous people. National radio and other media introduces new ideas that the members appropriate or reject as suitable for Christian worship which is prompted, encouraged, or dissuaded by their instructors, peers, or cultural dynamics.

Although music reading and writing was introduced by some missionaries and in select educational institutions, most people learn music through oral tradition.[7] This is so highly developed that it is possible to train a choir to sing by ear all kinds of complicated music if the instructors have a good understanding of the style. Christian

6.2 Drawing from oral tradition, Helen Mtawali trains Daystar University short-course students to sing the Lord's Prayer.

music is learned in school, in church, and church-related or church-affiliated gatherings and activities. These contexts include prayer or open-air gatherings, rituals, and sociocultural functions, such as funerals or political party gatherings, where Christian music is invoked either from radio and other audio and video recordings, on the street in urban areas, or just about any desirable venue. Thus there are formal learning situations with structured rehearsals and specific teachers and informal formats for acquiring music knowledge in ordered and controlled ways or in less exacting contexts. Instructors have been pastors, priests and missionaries, school teachers, parents, siblings and relatives, song leaders, choir leaders or members, and small ensemble music group members, such as worship teams. But learning also takes place from audio and video recordings. This broad base often makes it difficult to monitor and manage the music a denomination or group seeks to promote, even though it exposes members to a broad spectrum of repertoire. In this way, indigenous teaching and learning methods have been supplemented by ideas from neighboring and national cultures and the global market.

Musical Genres and Ensemble Types
Vocal and Choral Music

Congregational song is by far the most embraced and popular practice of musicking.[8] Hymnals were introduced as part of literacy projects, but most people learn new songs by rote through continuous use in different contexts and by different ensemble types. The most popular type of group ensemble is the choir.[9] Although choirs may service the church every Sunday, some are set up as a way to disciple or bond an age or gender group. Others are created for evangelistic purposes, for special occasions, such as weddings or Christmas, or they are created as a fundraising agency.[10] Some of the largest and most diverse choirs extant in one church are found in the Congo—*kwaya ya wamama, ya wazee, ya mayouth, ya kanisa* (Kiswahili for Mother's choir, Elder's choir, Youth Choir, Church choir). A choir can have as few as twelve members. Other types of ensembles may be small groups created for similar purposes, as outlined previously, or family or peer groups. These groups may have between two and twelve members, but they are often referenced as a choir. Choirs and small ensemble performances include traditional hymns, African hymns, gospel hymns, songs, and choruses.

6.3 *Small ensemble choir in the Democratic Republic of the Congo.*

In many cases melodies are harmonized. Currently, one of the most dominant ensemble types in some urban areas is the worship team, which is a global trend practiced in Africa as well as elsewhere in the world. These teams normally have a lead singer—referred to as a worship leader backed by a few singers or a choir. Accompaniment includes contemporary global instruments, such as synthesizers, guitars, or drum set. Although the primary repertoire are contemporary songs, hymns, and choruses of African and other origin, classic hymns or their arrangements are also performed as desired. The gospel music industry not only includes these various ensembles, but also the place of the solo, or lead singer, is greatly enhanced.

Instrumental Music and Music with Instruments

Instrumental music is possibly the least developed in the church in Africa. Missionaries initially banned almost all African instruments because they were considered pagan or associated with pagan rituals, or the playing and tuning styles were not conducive to the Christian musics introduced. In addition, missionaries did not know how to play these instruments to recommend their use. Therefore African instruments were publicly condemned, or new converts deemed them unsuitable because they had initially been excluded in the repertoire and stylistics introduced as Christian. The earliest instruments introduced were the organ for high churches, accordions, drums—whether side drums from Salvation Army practice or African drums appropriated as signals or metric markers—and some percussion. Beginning in the late 1950s, guitar (local variants or imports) grew to be extremely popular as radio became a primary disseminator of the Christian message, and popular music from the rest of the world and different African countries gained notoriety. The piano was introduced in some urban churches.[11] More recently, particularly from the 1980s, synthesizers, keyboards, and soundtracks are almost commonplace in gospel music and younger generation urban churches. Apart from some experiments by missionaries and the injunction by the Second Vatican Council in 1962 to include African melodic instruments, few are currently used in Christian circles in Africa. In some cases, African melodic instruments are introduced either as a novelty or for difference by gospel musicians or in arrangements of African tunes or compositions by African academic elites.

Popular or jazz band instruments have become fixtures for congregational singing. In urban areas where the congregation can afford these types of instruments, members of choirs and worship teams can and want to play them. At first the lead, rhythm, and bass guitars formed the backbone of the ensemble. Drums were sidelined or given subordinate roles as a metronome or time line instead of their instigating and communicative role in their parent culture groups. In some cases, new types of drums were introduced as surrogates— different in shape and technique from those in indigenous African practices. In time, syncretism of musical ideas has occurred relative to the piece of music. In some cases, indigenous drums and drum styles are incorporated, whereas in others, new types of drums with imposed roles or new drum techniques are created from a fusion of several different musical ideas (from indigenous African to church traditional to popular).

From the late 1950s to the 1970s, few European instruments, apart from those mentioned, were used. The exception was the Salvation Army who had brass bands and tambourines. Some urban or state churches sometimes incorporated European orchestral instruments in their anthems. With the growth of the choral and gospel music industry, instruments, such as trumpets or saxophones, began

6.4 Senufo one-string harp used in worship.

to appear in music recordings or even in churches. In time, not only instruments, but also music styles considered secular popular were appropriated. Reggae and rap are commonplace and even seminal in some gatherings. Since the early 1990s, it is as normal to find any assortment of instruments encouraged by the pastors, priests, or leaders as it is to find different types of music from a variety of sources in a church service or gathering with Christian "overtones," such as a wedding or send-off party.

MANAGING THE RELIGIOUS POPULAR MUSIC PRODUCT

In my research analysis of the music industry, the primary difference between a contemporary gospel musician or choir and a secular popular musician or group working within the same genre is the

6.5 *Daystar University faculty on retreat in Moro River, Kenya, worshiping with an assortment of instruments.*

lyrical content and maybe the motor or dance choreography. The church has been a primary training ground for singers who might be nurtured in congregation song or identified as good vocalists and encouraged to join the choir or a more specialized ensemble. They might even be afforded an opportunity to perform special songs in the services or in crusades. Timidity is quickly lost in such a public learning space, which is similar to what happens in indigenous pedagogy. These singers may choose to have more lessons or associate with different kinds of groups in which they learn new repertoire and more techniques. With or without encouragement, some of them record their output for sale or posterity. Thus there has always been a steady supply of singers from the congregation who make up the choir and other ensemble positions at any given time.

The same has not been true of instrumentalists. By the 1970s, there were few instrumentalists in the church beyond organists, pianists, and drummers—particularly church or indigenous drums. It was not uncommon for a church choir to invite a secular musician to their recording sessions. The advent of the synthesizer and availability of video samples that demonstrated the possibilities of different instruments changed the climate. The church became the training ground for aspiring instrumentalists. In some cases, the church owned the only available instruments and provided a regular playing gig, the Sunday service. A promising student could practice before a live audience in real time, in which he or she gained confidence and experience, and impressed or was forgiven by sympathetic congregants. Many churches tend to stay with one style of music for a long time. With some experience, these learners either move on to a different church and learn a new repertoire and styles or join other kinds of groups that challenge their technique, knowledge, and musicianship. This nomadic crop of musicians is therefore trained and reinforced in the church. They also spread the techniques or stylistics they have learned from one denomination or context to another. Often pastors will be glad to have a keyboardist or other musician to help attract members or contemporize their flock, and they hope that the musician will train some of the congregation's members to continue playing after he or she leaves. Because this group is made up of younger congregants, a church's musical repertoire can be transformed quite unexpectedly or rather subtly, depending on the knowledge and proficiency of the musician.

The growth and development of gospel or Christian music as a commercial product has created a market for singers and instrumentalists. In fact there is an increasing number of musicians whose sole

6.6 *Youthful musicians serve a church in the Democratic Republic of the Congo.*

profession is in this industry.[12] Recording, per se, is not necessarily for commercial benefit. Some musicians record as a way of copyrighting their compositions because notation is not a widespread means of asserting ownership. A musician can copyright lyrics, melody, style, or arrangement in this way. Recording may also be a means for posterity so that the group or person has in their possession some kind of documentation of their output and time together. Many choir groups take this route and pay to have just enough copies made for the members. Although some people might make a recording for commercial purposes, it is increasingly clear in some urban centers that young people, working particularly in gospel rap, find it a venue to air their views, thinking, opinions, let off steam, and testify. There are few avenues for this age group to have the ear of their peers and elders in multicultural and diverse nation-states. These artists will make a single and seek airtime at popular radio stations. If their product is successful, they might consider making more products or be approached for more songs. Often they make just that one recording and move on. Unfortunately for most of them, their elders rarely listen to the music because of the style in which it is couched. In some cases, it is not even considered worshipful. The music industry, however, has become one of the main teachers of music and its stylings through their products on radio and television and has introduced audiences not just to new songs, but also to new ways of doing Christian music.

MUSIC TRAINING

Few institutions have been set up to train musicians to work in the church. When I was asked to teach music in Bible schools in the 1980s to 1990s, I was expected to include some European music theory. Although it had little practical value for prospective church leaders, theory historically denoted literacy. Teaching of instruments was an uphill task because many rural churches had none or few instruments. They also held an ambivalent attitude toward African instruments. Youth were interested in participating in the global culture and preferred to learn keyboard or guitar to African instruments except for special choral numbers. Drums and other percussion instruments were accepted, but seminarians hoped the village or church had volunteer instrumentalists. Seminaries and Bible schools are so aware of the prevalence of music that they rarely train their students to be church musicians. This is a double-edged sword. Music is taken for granted in church as much as it is in the daily life of the African. Therefore a musician's training is approached in the same manner, through and by the community to identify and provide space to cultivate talent. Changes in music professionalism and the proliferation of theological positions reiterated through song, call for training of church musicians, or a more deliberate music education for pastors, priests, seminarians, and church workers. Because Christian music is approached as functional, the place and context for musical activities for Christians needs to be addressed and perhaps resolved so as to help producers and consumers deal with the intersection of the aesthetic, the technical, the ritual, the spiritual or religious, and the Christian in music.

OBSERVATIONS

There is clearly a product posited and marketed as Christian music in Africa. Its components are not fixed but are rather an aggregate of past musical experiences from the continent and beyond, embracing contemporary local and global trends. Congregational songs are most prevalent with a majority of female participants led mainly by men. Apart from congregational song, choirs, small ensembles, and soloists also thrive, serving different needs from pure evangelism to academic experiments to commercialism. Although music is defined mainly as sound from a Eurogenic position, African practitioners expand this framework to include other arts, motion, and spectacle (Stone 1998a, 7–12). The most prevalent African instruments in this music are membranophones and idiophones. The most common contemporary instrument is the guitar in its variants, but synthesizers and keyboards are part of the religious musicscape. Few instrumentalists play band, orchestral, and African melody instruments in Christian religious gatherings.

Christian and religious song has, at times, replaced indigenous songs in cultural ritual space. The learning and performance of this music in any space is mainly rooted in African methods of community public instruction where talent is recognized and encouraged. Thus the primary space for communal music making in Christianized Africa is the religious space. Therefore it also becomes the space for indigenous enculturation and discussion for those who embrace this faith. Thus the lyrics of spiritual songs or hymns may be social, historical, or political in content. For example, a gospel rapper may consider their composition a safe place to air their political and social views and not be considered dissident because gospel is considered a positive message whereas rap is associated with political and social discourse. Although the work might be aired on public radio or as a "special" in a gathering, it may not become part of the canon of community works, but its intended message will have been communicated. The creation of Christian music may be individual, but its acceptability and dissemination is public. Although the community may be the primal managers, religious leaders, song directors, and more recently, studio producers have become the most important administrators of the process and product.

As a note, the thief whose story begins this chapter did not find a way to fit into the Christianized culture. His cultural position and all it entailed, including being the village's official spy, had no place in the new social and religious understanding. But his song was incorporated into the congregational repertoire.

FOR DISCUSSION

1. Identify the different types of music used in the life of the African church. How were they introduced? Do missionaries (European, African, or other) use the same methods to introduce music considered Christian? Why or why not? What are the other methods through which new songs are encountered?

2. What kinds of teaching about music, musicianship, or musicians were given to African adherents? What was considered biblical and what was considered church or denominational doctrine or position?

3. What has been the impact of the music industry on music production and consumption in the church?

4. Do people need training to be effective in music ministry? Why or why not? How was such training done in Africa, if at all? How is this training done in your own environment, if at all?

5. Should pastors and other leaders receive training about music or even be trained as musicians? Why or why not?

6. CLASS PROJECT: Do a survey of Christian churches and institutions in your country about the type of training for church musicians. In your research and final report discuss the kind of teaching about music, musicianship, musicians, and Christianity that should be done to, and by, pastors, leaders, and congregants.

7

Bible
Lex Canendi, Lex Credendi

Roberta R. King

> *To sing once is to pray twice.*
>
> —Augustine[1]

She was a hard-working African woman. A former sorceress, Nonyime, had become one of the most renowned Christian singers among the Baptist churches in the Korhogo region of Côte d'Ivoire. Indeed, when Senufo people heard she was coming to sing at their local Christmas fête, believers and nonbelievers alike hurried from town and surrounding villages. In the midst of the communal festivities—complete with rice, peanut gravy, clapping, and dancing—the people were attracted most to the song lyrics, which were valued as treasures of biblical truth and wisdom. Two of Nonyime's most popular songs recounted the story of Job and the life of Christ, each expandable in length but usually lasting forty minutes in duration. Now, on this particular evening, Nonyime was interacting with a newly translated portion of scripture, Hebrews 11. She stood up in the midst of the local congregation. Drawing from a well-known proverb, she began her homily in song proclaiming, "Faith is like an egg . . . People, grab hold of faith!" The people turned their listening ears to hear these new reflections from the Scriptures. They could not afford to miss a word.

In the history of the Western church, worship studies declare, *lex orandi, lex credendi*: how one prays is how one believes. In the African church, the maxim shifts more to *lex canendi, lex credendi*: how one sings is how one believes. In other words, African Christian songs shape a people's faith. What is sung becomes a people's everyday working theology. As an essential means for processing life and communicating critical information, song with its wedding of appropriate musical style and verbal text forms a collaborative facilitation of social processes and cognitive understandings. Theologians posit that "culture is the workplace of Christian theology" (Walls 1996, 146). When African music systems are viewed as cultural product, it follows that song provides a locus for interacting with foundational questions about the Christian faith. Translated thus into the life of the African church, song composing processes foster major arenas for theologizing and for the spiritual formation of believers. The Bible serves as foundation and source of African Christian songs, a workplace of theology. This chapter looks at the dynamic integration of the biblical message within African contexts from three perspectives: the historical setting, oral foundations of African song, and musical encounters with the Scriptures.

Musical Encounters within the Church: Calls for Change

Historically, music in the life of the church in sub-Saharan Africa has been fraught with difficulties and misunderstandings. The introduction of Western hymns into the church reflected the mission practice of bringing one's own culture along with the gospel message. Christianity came packaged in foreign cultural containers. In the twentieth century, the foreignness of the gospel was maintained through the continued imposing of foreign and unintelligible music in the Church. Although Western hymns were sung well, they were not meaningful for many and did not speak to their life situations. African scholars and church leaders began to decry the situation. Calling for change, they argued that:

> If churches in Africa are to grow as African churches and not as extensions of parishes and bishoprics as some of them are now, then they must be allowed to take root in the soil of African culture in which they are planted, so that they may grow in stature as institutions of our own. (Nketia 1958, 268)

Thus there arose a yearning among African believers to know God within their own African context, that is, to allow the Christian faith to be at home in Africa. In Western Kenya, for example, a new way of religious life emerged as believers sought to no longer feel like strangers in their places of worship. Rather, they longed to "feel

7.1 Africa Israel Ninevah processing in downtown Nairobi.

at home."[2] Influenced by the revival in East Africa in the 1930s and 1940s, faith communities broke away from radically different church traditions and from Anglican to Pentecostal mission work. Resentment ran deep as new independent churches emerged.[3] One of the main reasons for dissent was the perception of an "attempt, if not of the early missionaries, at least of their more recent successors, to transplant the Church of England, lock, stock, and barrel, into African soil" (Welbourn and Ogot 1966, 4–5). This break away resulted in the exploration and introduction of African liturgical forms. Lengthy outdoor processions with the faithful dressed in white uniforms, carrying flags, singing in the vernacular, beating drums, and dancing served as witness to the larger community. Shouts of "Halleluiah" marked believers' entrance into the church, which believers perceived as the sacred domain (Welbourn and Ogot 1966).

After independence from mission churches, African Christians began singing the Christian faith in culturally appropriate ways. Although the church continued to sing some Western hymns as a part of their Christian heritage, the dynamics of worship shifted dramatically when believers turned to their own local hymns. Observers have noted the striking contrasts between the two Christian music worship styles:

> There they may sing hymns drawn from the books of the neighboring missions; they sing them sitting and with no more enthusiasm than an English village church. It is when they break into their own hymns that the change takes place and one feels that David, with his whole being is dancing before the Lord. These are based normally *on a biblical phrase* sung to a melody arising from the natural rhythm and intonation of the spoken words. They require a leader with a chorus, which uses complicated cross-rhythms of a most definite pattern. (Welbourn and Ogot 1966, 99; italics mine)

Significantly, the desire to know God through the biblical scriptures remained strong, even though the forms of worship had changed. As a result of contextualizing African worship patterns, the gospel was no longer being transplanted in superficial ways but was taking root in the soils of Africa. Liturgical practices significant to local people, such as singing in the mother tongue, dressing appropriately, and drawing from musical cultures that required clapping and dancing, became the norm. Such authentic engagement with the Scriptures via music was grounded in communication patterns inherent in oral cultures.

ORAL FOUNDATIONS OF AFRICAN CHRISTIAN MUSIC

Oral dynamics inherent in African song foster an environment for theologizing and embedding the Christian faith in the soil of Africa. Among their multiple functions, songs provide opportunities for processing life's vagaries, difficulties, and daily interactions (Nketia 1974, 189). Often incorporating the wisdom of proverbs, parables, and story, song texts address and offer advice about daily life issues. A gospel song from East Africa, for example, takes the biblical story of Paul and Silas as starting point and then offers advice:

> Paul and Silas prayed and the prison doors burst open.
>
> When you are tested, tried and you are overwhelmed by troubles
>
> Temptations and trials are overwhelming,
>
> Don't forget to pray, God will hear.
>
> Pray fervently like Paul and Silas. (Kidula 1998, 175)

Songs are highly valued as a major method for transmitting significant messages, both religious and nonreligious. The strength of song is that it weaves together musical sounds with verbal text within contemporary cultural settings. Enjoyable and entertaining as music is, the lyrical message is just as important and, at times, the most important component of a music performance.

Within this framework of oral tradition, composing African Christian songs offers a major arena for theological reflection and promotes the creation of a storehouse of theology (Hiebert 1985, 161–62). Musical orality consists of five key patterns that facilitate meaningful interaction with the biblical text.

1. **The call-and-response form**: African song forms readily move beyond a simple imitative format (a-a, b-b) to a highly complex set of varying lengths of calls and responses within any one given song. Lyrically, the various combinations of short and long responses depend on the relationship between text, tune, and text load. The performance of the call-and-response form, with its cyclical format, fosters an interdependent relationship between the lead singer(s) and the responding group. It allows for extending or adapting the text in ways that address new life issues.[4]

2. **Participation is essential**: As a result of its interdependent call-and-response form, participation in song is assumed and expected. The responding group becomes involved with the song and its text as the group relates with one another, often functioning as a bonding and identity-forming agent.

3. **Communal in orientation**: "I am because we are; and since we are, therefore I am" (Mbiti 1970, 189): it is in the group that people find their identity. This is demonstrated in African musical performances. Songs are most often sung in some form of group or ensemble in which the lead singer is dependent on a responding group coming in at the proper time before expounding on the text.

4. **Repetition valued**: Oral societies practice a high degree of repetition that guarantees memorable learning. Repetition also facilitates the singing of lengthy narratives in which repeated responses focus attention and return the group to the main theme of the song.

5. **Aggregative development of the text**: The content of a song develops over a longer period of musical performance to communicate its full message. Psalm 136, for example, reflects an

oral pattern in which every other phrase is the response, "His love endures forever." As the song progresses, the narrative of the text grows and develops in an accumulative fashion with each successive addition.

These oral features influence and shape African Christian music as ethnic groups draw from their oral heritage and proven means of communication. When free to interact with the Scriptures in musical settings, the biblical message is integrated into the musical culture in appropriate ways. The musical arena is prepared for receiving the word of God in a way that fosters theologizing in context.

Musical Encounters with Scripture: Emerging African Theologies

How then does the Bible serve as foundation and source of the church's music? What are the emerging oral theologies arising within the contexts of the African church? The response is vast and highly varied. In general, the more Scriptures that believers learn, the greater the amount of scripture that is included or alluded to in song, especially when translated Scriptures are made available. The discussion now turns to three illustrative church groups, each one representing a differing church tradition.

Searching for Biblical Truth

In 1913, the first seeds were planted by William Wade Harris, a Liberian evangelist-cum-prophet, for what would become the Harrist Church among the Dida people of south-central Côte d'Ivoire. In eighteen short months of evangelistic ministry, a mass movement estimated between one hundred thousand and two hundred thousand people from among the Dida and at least a dozen other ethnic groups turned "from traditional religious beliefs and practices toward a new reality structured around certain rudimentary tenets of the Christian faith as prescribed by the Prophet" (Krabill 1995, v). Although Harris had presented "the Book" to the new Dida believers during his short sojourn, it was impossible for the non-literate leaders and congregants to access the written Scriptures. In essence they were "largely cut off from the Book that contained the teachings of God's prophets and of His Son Jesus-Christ" (Krabill 1995, 365). Dida believers processed and incorporated increased amounts of biblical truth into their local hymns as they gained more access to the scriptures. From 1913 to 1949, gathering up bits and pieces of the biblical message from wherever possible, Harris believers sang the Scriptures as soon as they could learn them. One preacher, for example, regularly learned Bible stories from a local shopkeeper who had come from Sierra Leone. Immediately explaining them to an assembled choir in his courtyard, they were transformed into songs for use in worship. Biblical references in the early hymns include the creation of the world, the temptation of Job, the wisdom of Solomon, John the Baptist, Christ's coming to earth, Christ's healing ministry (Mark 5:25-34), Christ's teaching (Matt 11:28), Christ's death and resurrection, Christ's reign on Mount Zion, return of Christ, last judgment, and heaven and hell (Krabill 1995, 366).

Harrist hymns progressively became more informed by biblical tradition, often showing an affinity with the Psalms.

> I want to follow my God.
>
> I give Him all the things in my heart.
>
> I call upon God, I call upon God;
>
> That He might hear and understand my mouth in His mercy.
>
> Yes, I walk with the strong heart of my God.
>
> I do war in the midst of those who are against me.
>
> My enemies encircle me.
>
> My God, come close to me.
>
> And remove me from sin. (Krabill 1995, 367)

As the hymn corpus emerged, several theological themes came to the fore, among them the following dominant ones.[5]

Toward an African Christology

The Dida hymns are representative of early African perceptions of Jesus Christ. Scholars have bemoaned a crisis in written African Christologies.[6] Yet through oral tradition, Dida believers exemplify a Christological confidence "operative among indigenous believers ever since Christianity arrived on the continent" (Stinton 2004, 4). For example, chief among Dida early priorities was learning to know a new "big brother," a common theme arising across the continent, from Ghana to Kenya and Uganda (Stinton 2004, 146–52). Overall, the early Dida hymns answer the question of "who Jesus is" by bestowing on him "honorific" titles, such as king, lord, wise one, and handsome. They also refer to Jesus as a family member, such as father, son, offspring, and brother. The range of Christological perceptions broadens to many areas, including an emphasis on healing by referring to Jesus as "the First-Medicinal-Grinding Stone" and "Medicine-For-Our-Troubled-Deeds." In later years, as believers have become better acquainted with the Scriptures, terms are more biblically informed, referring to Jesus as the true vine, good shepherd, and so on. They also identify Jesus' earthly origins, Nazareth, Galilee more clearly, and highlight how he "speaks truth, sustains, tends, guards, etc." (Krabill 1995, 370–71).

African Perceptions of God

The Dida, who acknowledged the existence of God before the coming of Harris, grew theologically into a new and fuller understanding of the God they had always known, though perhaps more vaguely. Relating this in a hymn, they explain, "We knew that God had made us, that He had placed us on this earth . . . but we did not understand His affair" (Krabill 1995, 372).

Among the new understandings about God and most often cited references to God in the hymn corpus are two especially dominant

7.2 William Wade Harris with a convert and four women singers of faith.

ones, that of "father" and "life-renewer." Drawing close to the formerly distant, creator God who has now come close is stated thus:

> We too, we have at last found our Father.
>
> We did not know that we were going to find our Father.
>
> But we have found our Father;
>
> Our Father is our King of Glory. (Krabill 1995, 375)

Similarly, there is a wonderful note of surprise in the following text about God as life-renewer:

> Ayi wowo,[7] the Lord gave birth to us, you!
>
> The Life-Renewer, the Doer-of-Good gave birth to us!
>
> We did not know
>
> That the Lord was going to give birth to us two times! (Krabill 1995, 375)

These two texts reveal the integrating of new information into the Dida's worldview.

Last Things

Harrist hymns show a movement from the concept of "the village of the dead" to heaven and hell. Harris warned that a day was coming when God would destroy the earth and forest with fire. Eschatological discourse of the hymns reflects a major portion of Harris's message in which more than eighty hymns reference topics about the last days, among them are references to a great trial that will take place. The "last judgment" discourse in Matthew 25:31–46 is alluded to in hymns that tell how the faithful ones with "the sign of the cross" traced on believers' foreheads at baptism will receive a "fresh and peaceful heart." On the other hand, the unfaithful will "go into the village of fire and suffering." In a later hymn, the hymn writer translates almost literally the full text of the biblical passage (Krabill 1995, 378).

Thus the Dida Harrists reveal how an indigenous, independent church group naturally took the Christian message and how they interacted with the biblical text and developed an oral theology expressed in song. Two domains, that of culture or worldview and the biblical message, are interwoven in ways that process the Christian faith into their daily life context through song. Mission-based churches, on the other hand, have approached integrating the Christian faith in different ways and at different starting points.

Knowing God through the Translated Word

Not all mission church planting efforts have maintained allegiance to Western hymns in the church in Africa. For example, among Senufo believers in the north of Côte d'Ivoire, the singing of hymns literally put the agricultural field workers to sleep, both in musical style and in unintelligible content. Such dire circumstances in the 1950s forced pursuing the development of an indigenous, culturally appropriate hymnody (King 1989, 92–116). Linked with the growth of indigenous hymnody was receiving the Gospel of Mark as their first translated book in 1960. Amazed to have God's word speaking directly to them in their own language, a people movement arose. Indigenous Senufo Christian songs began springing up.

Over time, national church leaders and missionaries alike observed a fixation on songs of testimony that developed more reflection on the acts of Satan in believer's former lives, than what it meant "to walk the Jesus road" as Senufo Christians.[8] National believers, especially women, who are the song composers in the culture, developed an appropriate form that allowed for a high degree of content and narrative singing. Senufo Baptists turned to making songs drawn from the Scriptures. Linked with the translation of the Bible, Senufo believers grew theologically as they incorporated them into song.[9]

Among the findings, analysis of the song texts revealed a dynamic interaction between two streams of consciousness: Senufo worldview and an evolving biblical theology. For example, the song text, "Faith is Like an Egg" opens with a well-known cultural proverb. The composer encourages and admonishes believers based on the metaphor of the fragility of an egg by warning people to handle their faith with careful attention. At the same time, she also develops her reflections from the biblical passage, Hebrews 11:5. Concrete examples of bad conduct enumerated in the song point to the breaking of Senufo values, that is, "the activities of a disobedient child, of living one's life as one pleases without regard for the rest of society, the lack of respect for others, of stubbornness towards others" (King 1989, 392). Such actions turn people in the wrong direction, triggering a fall or a "breaking" of faith, one that is not pleasing to God. In essence, the song asks, how do we please God? and discusses

---

FAITH IS LIKE AN EGG (BASED ON HEBREWS 11:5)

Opening Thematic Statement:

People, grab hold of faith!
Faith is like an egg. If it escapes and falls, it breaks.
People, grab hold of faith!

Repeated Response:

People, grab hold of faith!

Development/Exegesis:

1. Faith is like an egg. If it escapes and falls, it breaks.
2. It is because of faith that God raised up Enoch.
3. It is because of faith that Peter walked on the water.
4. You cannot please God without faith.
5. No one can please God without faith.
6. There are the things of the world that you are looking at. And if faith escapes and falls . . .
7. There is the money of the world that you are looking at. And if faith escapes and falls . . .
8. It is the bad behavior (of a person) that you are looking at. And if faith escapes and falls . . .
9. There are the good-looking men of the world that you are looking at. And if faith escapes and falls . . .
10. There are the beautiful women of the world that you are looking at. And if faith escapes and falls . . .

Closing Thematic Statement:

People, grab hold of faith!
Faith is like an egg. If it escapes and falls, it breaks.
People, grab hold of faith! (King 1989, 315)

---

immoral values that lead people away from God. The lives of Enoch and Peter, including his walking on water, are exposited in the full narrative of the song; they become models of faith. Senufo believers in Christ are thus encouraged to faithfully follow the "Jesus Road."

The interaction between Scripture, worldview, and the Christian life is consistent throughout the young, emerging hymn corpus. Similar to the Dida, prominent theological themes for the Senufo center on "who Jesus is," referring to him as lord, our father Jesus Christ, the giver of freedom, the one who heals, the author of love,

7.3 Nɔnyime, *composer of the song, "Faith is Like an Egg" trains song leaders to sing from the Scriptures.*

ancestor, and the owner of heaven—"his village." They also focused on "what God has done" by noting their freedom from bad works and "the bad things of Satan," creating the earth, giving Jesus to die for them and showing his love (King 1989, 209–39). Worldview and Christian life issues center on turning from animistic worship (fetishes) to freedom in Christ. Repeated concerns include maintenance of balance between the natural and the supernatural realms, maintenance of justice between neighbors and other people, and dealing with personal problems relating to moral conduct, attitudes, and physical conduct (King 1989, 192–204).

Clinging to Christ in Tough Times

Local theologies, that developed in song across the continent, vary in starting point. The Episcopal Church of Sudan, which has known great persecution over a long period of time, is "creating contextual songs out of a need to cling to something which might give them security amidst the chaos of displacement" (Campbell 2003, 2). Among Dinka believers there exists a plethora of songs concerning Christ's sacrificial shedding of blood. Blood, covenant, and sacrifice play major roles in the Dinka culture: "In order to make a covenant with someone, blood must be shed. In order to heal someone, they must be covered with blood. The shedding of blood ties the community more tightly together [creating a cultural] connection between this and the act of communion" (Campbell 2003, 7).

Thus Dinka believers are in a strong position to understand the concept of the atonement as a result of their cultural practices in living out covenant, as the following song illustrates:

> We are washed by the blood of Christ
>
> And yet we turn back to the wrong,
>
> Past things that we have done.
>
> We reach to you, Lord save us,
>
> We have called upon you.
>
> —Peter Matiop Chol 1995 (Campbell 2003, 7)

Because covenant is taken seriously, song composers have chosen to refer to the shedding of Christ's blood, which in their eyes seals the covenant, as the main form of appeal against sin (Campbell 2003, 7). Interacting faithfully with the Scriptures, they have begun their theologizing at the point they find most relevant to their life

7.4 Dinka women of Sudan sing their faith with crosses in hand on Palm Sunday.

experience. They are then well placed to move on to preaching the full gospel in those arenas of life that are not perceived as immediately relevant yet necessary. The process of theology making, though slow, spirals forward, suggesting a hermeneutical method.

THEOLOGIZING IN SONG AS HERMENEUTICAL METHOD

As African believers have interacted with the Scriptures through song they have begun the critical process of bringing the God of the Bible into their life contexts. The long-trumpeted call for bringing the gospel message home to the soil of Africa takes place within the music-making processes of the church. As seen previously, whether in West, Central, or East Africa and irrespective of church tradition, African musicking fosters an integrative process of theological and creative contextualization in which the biblical text is processed via an expressive cultural form, that of African song.

Thus the process of theologizing in song (see figure 7.5) suggests a hermeneutical method that draws from practices embedded in a people's culture. Working within their local cultural context, African music-making processes gather together multiple streams of daily life concerns confronting African believers. Then, functioning as a hermeneutical community, believers transform their reflections into song as they consider daily life issues in light of the biblical text. The biblical message aligned with critique of the culture and addressing needed responses to the God of the Bible becomes the central concern as songs are composed. Thus an emerging African theology is expressed in lyrical form. The process is not stagnant, but dynamic. Progressively cyclical in practice, new songs arise out of

7.5 The Cyclical Process of Theologizing in Song.

further interaction with the Scriptures, maturing perceptions about God, and new life issues.

African Christian Songs in the Global Church

As the African church moves into the global arena in the twenty-first century, it naturally continues to draw from its music-making systems with which it is familiar, both in terms of musical culture and textual issues. Yet the church is at the same time responding in new, dynamic, and creative ways. Greater exposure to a wider variety of music heard on the radio, on audiocassettes and CDs, or downloaded off the Internet creates new musical interests for African Christian composers. This is especially true among urban youth. As one Kenyan music teacher explained, "Music is anything that interests you in sound."[11] New musical interests incorporate electronic instruments known and played worldwide. Yet this does not necessarily, and nor should it, negate rich aspects of African musical heritage; new instruments can be, and are, played in African ways. Above all, whether in the village, town, cities, or in Diaspora, there remains the penchant to interact with the Scriptures in relevant and meaningful ways via song in ways that continue to foster bringing God into the midst of daily African life. Drawing from inherited music traditions, African Christian composers offer to the global church new ways of engaging with God on a more expansive scale. Among them is a process for theologizing in song that looks to the Scriptures in ways that integrate and confront contemporary issues. What one sings will continue to shape and inform what one believes: *lex canendi, lex credendi.*

For Discussion

1. Identify and discuss how Western societies communicate orally in the twenty-first century? How do they differ from African societies?

2. Study ten song texts from popular culture. What issues and life concerns are they raising? Identify Christian songs that address these issues from a biblical perspective.

3. Find ten Christian songs in which scripture is used as a major component of the text. What is the major life question each song raises and what do we learn about God in each of them?

4. Psalm 136 is composed in a call-and-response song form. Read it together as a class in which half the room reads the changing text and the other half always speaks the refrain. Now make it into a rap by speaking and moving to it.

5. CLASS PROJECT: Create a theologizing-through-song class portfolio. Based on figure 7.5, identify five major contemporary concerns and issues that need to be addressed. Drawing from the Scriptures, write a series of psalms or songs that address these issues. Some people may write the text while others may choose to compose the music.[10]

8

Global Church
Lessons from Africa

Roberta R. King

You cannot do anything unless God is there.
—Ghanian proverb[1]

JONAH AND THE KEYBOARD

On the outskirts of Abidjan, Côte d'Ivoire, the weekend church conference was already in progress as I arrived. More than two hundred African believers were deeply engaged in listening to an exposition of the Scriptures. Just before they took a lunch break, the afternoon workshops were announced. The church leadership requested that people indicate which one they would attend by standing in different parts of the room. When they announced my workshop on music in the church, close to three-fourths of the group stood showing their intention to come discuss music. The leadership, somewhat disconcerted by the few numbers left to attend the remaining four alternative presentations, pleaded with and finally assigned several people to other workshops. Clearly music was central and important to this faith community.

As an outsider to the church and wanting to become acquainted with their music in worship, I began the seminar by asking the participants to sing a song that was especially meaningful to them. What ensued was a skirmish between two major musical groups. One group was made up of women lead singers, both rural and urban. Singing in parallel harmonies, they recounted the story of Jonah. The remainder of the workshop group joined in by singing the tightly interwoven responses, clapping intricate patterns, and ultimately standing to move to the complex rhythms that drove the story forward. Drawing from

133

oral tradition, the song was sung in their mother tongue and authentically derived from their ethnic tradition. The other group was led by young people who wanted to sing and incorporate the electronic keyboard into their music. I wondered to myself, would they sing a contemporary Christian worship song from the West? Did they know the history of encounter between Western Christianity and Africa? What should music in the global church look like?

In many ways, the story of music in the life of the African church is the story of innumerable cultural encounters. The encounter between people of two different cultural arenas, the West and Africa, has certainly made its mark on the African Church. The story of Jonah and the keyboard is yet another story of cultural encounter. Only this time, it takes place within the same culture. Differences in age form new contexts for encounter. In today's global world, cross-cultural encounters have expanded to include cross-generational encounters as the burgeoning church in Africa comes of age. The situation is not unique to Africa but is taking place around the world. It is a global issue in which both cross-cultural and cross-generational encounters are occurring simultaneously.

In the twenty-first century, music in the life of the African church in many places has become dynamic and full of vitality. In other parts

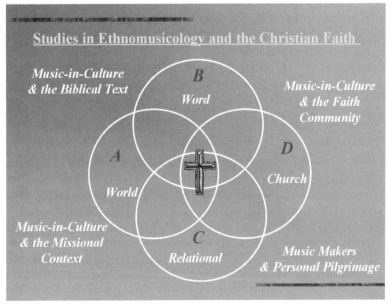

8.1 A matrix for studies in Global Church Music.

of Africa, there is still much more to do in terms of Christian witness and worship. This chapter discusses the dynamics of the contribution of music in witness and worship in the church in Africa. Many of these musical dynamics are not limited to Africa. In today's global reality, local churches in every context struggle with similar issues and concerns. Thus the purpose is to glean lessons and principles that nourish strong and vital faith communities wherever they are located. The questions raised are: What does music in the life of the African church teach us? What should music in the global church of the twenty-first century look like? What are the essential and constant dynamics between music, culture, and the gospel that form a foundational philosophy for music in the life of the global church?

These questions are considered framed around a matrix for studying global church music presented at the beginning of the study in chapter 1 (figure 1.5). It is made up of four interactive arenas between music-in-culture and the Christian faith: the Biblical text, the missional context, personal pilgrimage, and the faith

8.2 Senufo balafons (jegele) and drums announce the good news.

community. They coalesce in the midst of the music-making event, whenever and wherever music is made.

MUSIC AND THE MISSIONAL CONTEXT

The dynamic intersection between musical culture and the missional context can contribute significantly to the development of appropriate Christianity in which the faith is sung in culturally appropriate ways.

A missional context is created any time someone moves into a new or different culture. The differences may be great as when moving around the world or they may be more subtle as found in age differences or subcultural groupings within a larger cultural context. The missional context includes musical cultures that differ from one's own. Simply singing the same song in both cultures does not guarantee the same impact or understanding of the song. Thus singing the Christian faith in meaningful and appropriate ways within a new cultural context is paramount. It is important to note that singing the Christian faith in culture-specific ways, which create understanding of the Christian message, is not dependent on text only. As communicators of the gospel, the text forms the core element and provides the starting point. However the text must be appropriately wed with the musical culture of a people. When it is not, barriers to understanding the Christian message regularly interfere with knowing God within a people's specific cultural context. Musical sound, form, function, performance praxis, and text go hand in hand; they should not be divorced from one another. Translating a Western hymn into a new language or inserting Christian words on top of a local tune is not sufficient. Important principles to learn from the African church about musical cultures are now discussed.

Musical Cultures Are Organized Differently

With musical sound as a common starting point, each culture creates its own governing set of assumptions and rules about their music (Titon 2002, 17). Variations in acceptable sounds and instruments immediately strike outsiders as foreign or strange as they hear and experience another culture's music for the first time. Based on their own musical assumptions and expectations, Western missionaries to Africa often misjudged all music as pagan and heathen. They did not understand the important differences they encountered in the new musical spaces of Africa. For example, the centrality of music for negotiating life, especially major life events, places music at the locus of society. Significant messages are often sung rather than merely spoken. Deeply embedded thoughts and values are shared through song and the musical arts. At the same time, music in Africa is inseparably woven together with dance, drama, and spectacle in ways that heightens and fosters the teaching of significant thoughts and values on multiple levels. Behind the sound, dance, and drama of each music event lies deeper cultural realities. As Jean Kidula pointed out in chapter 3, in some African cultures the natural and supernatural are intertwined and related to such a degree that music is essential to negotiating various spiritual realities and must be present almost constantly. Thus music is a dominant part of both religion and daily life. As the church in Africa is maturing and bringing Christ deeper into their lives, music for worship and spiritual formation is becoming more appropriate and meaningful as believers discerningly incorporate essential and acceptable features of their musical cultures. Recognizing and working within a people's musical culture in appropriate ways can lead to making a significant difference in creating understanding of who Jesus Christ is. The church is recreating and reconfiguring the musical cultures for the purposes of the kingdom of God.

A CASE OF MUSICAL ETHNOCENTRISM

A twenty-year veteran American missionary among the Maasai recently attended a Maasai church service in Kenya. Joe had a degree in music and specialized in percussion instruments, among them drumming. The Maasai do not traditionally play drums, but drums were included at this service. Joe said, "The guy playing the drums was playing this very simple beat (really nothing but one beat after another; practically no rhythm or variation)." As he listened, Joe thought, "that drum beat is so basic, it just bugs me. It can be done a lot better without being offensive." So he asked, "Hey, could I try that?" He did, and he expanded the beat with a few simple additions. After a few minutes the Maasai drummer came back and said, "You don't know how to play the drums. Let me do it." It was quite the learning and humbling experience. Joe thought to himself, "Here is this guy from the bush telling me, a guy with a BA in music, that I can't play the drums simply because I don't duplicate his 'dull' pattern!" (E-mail correspondence with CMA missionaries, 2006)

Musical Ethnocentrism Should Not Impede Effective Communication of the Gospel through Music

It is important to recognize that each culture or subcultural grouping of people have cultural lenses that affect the way they evaluate or judge another people's music. The wholesale transplanting of Western Christian hymns to replace all assumed heathen and pagan music in many parts of Africa has led to innumerable misunderstandings of the gospel and poor relationships between people. Different sounds and performance practices, such as dancing, do not necessarily mean the same thing to both inside participants and outside observers. The church and musicians need to carefully reflect on and discern which musical sounds, styles, and practices will bring glory to God and make him known among the people within their own culture. Indeed, "the gospel is always distinct from, sometimes affirming of, and often prophetically critical of all human cultures" (Van Engen 2006a, 97). This is true of musical cultures as well; a person must learn to discern what is appropriate and what is not appropriate for each musical genre and cultural practice.

Musical Cultures Are Dynamic and Always Changing

For many people in Africa, "music is anything that interests you in sound."[2] Thus they are always using sounds drawn from their local sound environment. The global media has influenced musical composition in Africa, where musicians have chosen to weave into their music the sounds they have heard on the radio, television, and other sources. These new sounds appear to be most successful when they are brought into African music-making modes, rather than mere imitation of foreign music. This provides both continuity with the past and also fosters living in one's contemporary world.

MUSIC AND THE BIBLICAL TEXT

The thoughtful interaction between music-in-culture, particularly song, and the biblical text leads to dynamic singing of the Christian faith in meaningful ways.

Music facilitates the integration of daily life with the word of God in the lives of African believers within their local faith communities. As such, music serves as a life processor, a means for interacting with the biblical scriptures. It plays a central role in integrating the

Christian faith within a people's life context. However this has not always been the case. The church in sub-Saharan Africa has wrestled with appropriating Christianity in its widely diverse contexts. As one group of theologians stated, "[o]ur struggle, in brief, is not to Christianize our African traditions but to Africanize the Christian faith so that we understand and appreciate Christianity within our African context" (Nancy 1993, 4). Thus important principles related to music in the life of any church are discussed next.

Communication of the Gospel Message with Music that is Understood by People within Their Local Setting

The highest priority for the church is communicating the gospel through music that facilitates understanding and knowing God within a people's worldview. As Hiebert notes (1985, 55), "All authentic communication of the gospel . . . should be patterned on biblical communication and seek to make the Good News understandable within their own cultures."

The introduction of music from outside of one's culture, such as Western hymns in Africa, without understanding the new, local musical culture, led to misunderstanding of the Christian message. When one does not take time to understand a people's cultural music, it is easily misjudged. For example, many missionaries to Africa interpreted all African music:

> as heathen and immoral without trying to understand [the dances and music], what they were for and what significance they had in the life of the people to whom they had come to teach Christianity. (Temu 1972, 155)

If we do not employ music that is known and understood, foreign music will create numerous barriers to accepting and understanding the biblical text that people long to make known. The word remains wrapped in "plastic bags" and is inaccessible. As one Senufo woman in Côte d'Ivoire said when asked about a recently translated Western hymn, "What language is that song in?" (King 1989, 103). Expecting to hear an important message as practiced in her culture, she could not begin to understand the Good News presented in the song. Though it was a wonderful song in its original cultural setting, the song was meaningless to her. Both text and song genre are interwoven to create understanding; the relation of the text to the music is integral to fully comprehending the meaning of a song.

8.3 What music is most meaningful and appropriate for these believers in the Democratic Republic of the Congo?

Begin with What Does the Music Mean to the Receptor?

This is the question most often not asked by the church. Although people are welcome to listen to various music, including Christian music from around the world and enjoy their unique sounds, there is no guarantee that they will automatically understand the intended meaning of the music or message in a song. Speaking of music as a universal language often leads to the assumption that everyone makes sense of the music in the same way. However foreign musical systems remain meaningless when not understood, even though people may have repeatedly heard the music and participated in congregational singing or musical performances. Or as often happens, they attach a totally different meaning to a foreign music.

At the time of African independence movements in the 1960s, an East African scholar raised critical questions that are still pertinent for today:

> The choirs in churches in post-Uhuru[3] Africa continue singing meaningless holy songs. Has Christianity failed to inspire any poet to compose songs of praise to the Christian God? Or is the God of Christendom deaf to prayers spoken in the African medium? (p'Bitek 1973, 4)

Significantly, p'Bitek was not the only one experiencing the hymns as meaningless. He recognized that God, as the creator of the universe, was neither monolingual nor limited to one particular musical culture. Across the continent, various streams of African Christian music began rising up from their musical wellsprings.

The question: for whom is this music meaningful continues to be a major problem in the church worldwide. Or one could ask: How is a song or music understood? Unwittingly, the assumption has been that music already used elsewhere in the Christian church has become universally sacred. Indeed, it is sacred for a particular group of people. It is imperative, though, to recognize that meaning is located in the people who are hearing or participating in it. Meaning is also dependent on the language and context in which it is performed. Individual listeners and groups of people make the final decision on the meaning of a song or musical piece. Thus employing music that is contextually appropriate for specific groups of people must remain a top priority.

Contextualizing music requires composing songs locally within the African context. As Thomas Oduro pointed out in chapter 5, once the African church was free to make their own songs, African hymnodies and gospel songs became an effective agent in transmitting

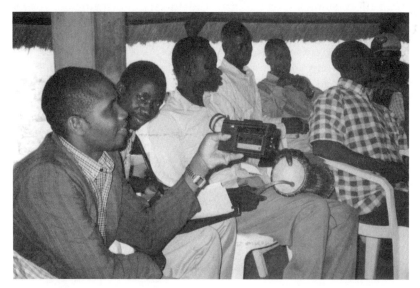

8.4 *Nyarafolo and Minyanka Senufo believers "capture" a new song that they have just composed in a New Song Fellowship workshop in Ferkessedougou, Côte d'Ivoire.*

the faith to Africans. Thus it is profoundly significant when he states, "Africans, these days, sing with meaning." Indigenous literary practices, including oral communication devices and African poetic forms, wed with musical styles that express a people's deep feelings in meaningful ways are foundational to creating appropriately contextualized Christian music that impacts the lives of believers.

Theological Reflection through Song Promotes Knowing God in Context

Many African theologians recognize that a major arena for theologizing takes place in the song making and music performance event. In fact, it is quite common for African believers to burst forth into song as they are testifying to the goodness of God in their lives. The practice arises out of the value of song carrying deep concepts about God's character and interactive work in their lives.

Composing new songs based on Scripture provides a platform for reflecting on the scriptures and how they interact with a specific cultural context. The process allows issues and concerns prevalent within someone's own unique cultural context to be raised in light of the Scriptures. Theologians have come to call this process of interacting with the scriptures in varying cultural contexts, contextualization. Stanley Grenz affirms the priority of bringing the gospel message home to each cultural group when he states that:

> Contextualization demands that the theologian take seriously the thought-forms and mindset of the culture in which theologizing transpires, in order to explicate the eternal truths of the Scriptures in language that is understandable to contemporary people. (Grenz 1993, 90)

The song composing process brings together culture-specific languages understandable to local people in ways that draw on their thought-forms and cultural mindset within the medium of musicking. Although most commonly thought of as a literary process, musical procedures in Africa and elsewhere provide a welcome arena for oral theological reflection in context. Music and text that is culture specific fosters knowing God in context, in deeply meaningful and authentic ways. What one sings, becomes what one believes.

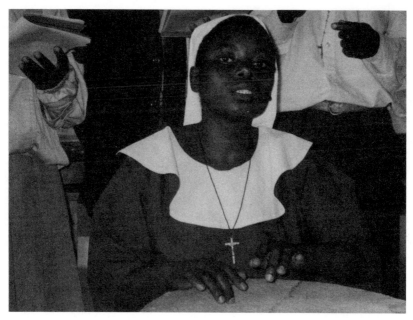

8.5 An AIC singer at a New Song Fellowship workshop in Kitale, Kenya.

MUSIC MAKERS AND PERSONAL PILGRIMAGE

The intentional interaction between Christian music makers with spiritual formation and disciplines will lead to the creation and use of Christian music that nourishes the life of the Church.

By acknowledging the central role that music plays in the life of the African church, both in terms of lyrical content and creating the appropriate atmosphere for worship and gospel communication, the discussion now considers the spiritual development of Christian musicians and the need to educate the managers of Christian music.

Christian Musicians Must Be Grounded in Biblical Knowledge, Spiritual Formation, Spiritual Disciplines, and Theological Reflection

In many places around the world, music is so prevalent in daily life that musicians are taken for granted. Indeed, as Kidula pointed out, "music is taken for granted in church as much as it is in the daily life of the African." Christian musicians need a well-rounded training that includes biblical knowledge, a theology of music, and the refining of theological reflection. This provides a theological foundation for guiding them as influential leaders in the Christian church.

Church Leadership Must Be Provided with a Theology and Philosophy of Music that Fosters Good Decision Making and Leadership Related to Christian Music in the Church

The managers of Christian music in the church are often people who have not been trained in music. They acknowledge and know that music is important but are limited to making decisions without a guiding theology of music or a philosophy of music in Christian worship, witness, and spiritual formation. Thus religious leaders, song directors, studio producers, and administrators of both the product and process will benefit from resources and seminars that provide theological guidance surrounding the many considerations related to Christian music.

Musicians Must Be Provided Space and Opportunity to Develop Musical Skills and Practice Composing Songs for the Church

Composing songs that faithfully transmit the Christian message requires the intentional development of musicians. The composing style may vary, from "catching songs," as practiced in AICs, to individual compositions and group composing. It is critical that musicians learn to make music by having space to explore, practice, and try out new musical ideas. When given opportunity to create new songs within an environment of encouragement, affirmation, and loving critique by Christian leaders and the Christian community, new songs can grow in musical expertise and theological depth. The Victorian era of hymn writers recognized this, and the result is that many of their four hundred thousand hymns continue to be sung around the world today.

MUSIC AND THE FAITH COMMUNITY

The intersection between appropriate musical culture and the Christian faith community, the church, contributes significantly to fostering spiritual growth in the love and knowledge of Jesus Christ and authentic worship "in spirit and in truth" (John 4:24).

AN UNTOLD MUSICAL STORY FROM THE RWANDAN GENOCIDE

Christian songs and hymns have played critical roles within the lives of African believers, especially during times of trial, persecution, and genocide. In 1994, in the midst of the slaughtering of more than 800,000 people in Rwanda, stories of faith and heroism also took place. One Hutu minister, who also had members of the Tutsi ethnic groups in his con-

Dynamic vitality and growth is a hallmark of the church in sub-Saharan Africa, especially because it is becoming more rooted in African soils. The growth of musical expression parallels the growth of a dynamic church that is both phenomenal and staggering. As the music has become more meaningful, it has played a profound role in the life of the church. The guidelines concerning music that the African church offers to the global church are discussed here.

gregation, worked at protecting them against the mindless killing targeted at them. Once this was discovered people from his own ethnic group turned on him, his wife, and five children. As the killers came to their home, the family sought refuge under the bed in the back bedroom. What did the family do in such dire circumstances? They sang Christian songs and hymns in praise of the God they had chosen to serve. The assasins never found them and their lives were spared. They are currently serving the African church today.

Pursue Developing and Employing Music that Builds the Faith of Christian Believers in Ways that Facilitate Utter Dependence on God

As African believers have struggled through political upheavals, civil wars, persecutions, and other devastating calamities, they have learned to cling to God, most often with a song on their lips. Music plays a profoundly central role in forming allegiance to God as people process life in their attempt to cope with the varying, often disconcerting, strands of life. The singing of Christian songs

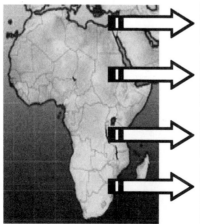

8.6 *Four Major Streams of Church Music in Africa.*

8.7 Nairobi Baptist Church choir on their journey of incorporating more African musical elements.

and hymns offers hope, protection, and renewed strength to survive. In Africa, listening to, participating in, and singing culturally appropriate songs provides comfort and assurance of God's omnipotence and goodness in the midst of life's vagaries and cruelties.

Respect Each Group of People within the Church and Their Musical Languages and Traditions

The immense diversity of languages and ethnicities on the African continent imposes the need to recognize and treat different people and their cultural patterns of living with respect. This is not easily done; many divisions between people still exist. However the church is leading the way as they embrace, recreate, and incorporate the multiple streams of musical heritage that form their unique history within their local setting.

Although church music in reality is a complex blend of many elements, a simplified schema shows that at least four major streams of church music are taking place in Africa (see figure 8.5). For example, it is not unusual to find churches in Nairobi, Kenya, singing the hymn, "My Hope is Built on Nothing Less" in four different ways: 1) as a Western hymn in the English language with the original Western tune, 2) as a gospel song with the text still sung in English but the musical style has been modified, 3) as a *pambio*[4] sung in Kiswahili in a Kenyan musical style with movements and dancing, and 4) a thoroughly vernacular song, in language, musical style, and with new text. The essential principle is that each church is becoming who they are in the Lord Jesus Christ by drawing from all that he has given them. They are creating their unique musical identity in Christ.

Create Christian Community through the Forming of Hermeneutical New Song Fellowships

Composing Christian songs in groups has become an important means for both planting and developing churches in Africa.[5] Working with groups of believers who share a common vernacular language provides opportunities to interact with the Scriptures in culturally informed ways. As they compose African-based songs that incorporate both theri vernacular language and music, the Christian faith becomes more appropriately rooted within their unique cultural context. An inclusive community grows because the method cuts through class divisions, especially between literate and non-literate, in which everyone within a particular language group is valued and is given opportunity to contribute their musical skills and their opinion. In addition, the method provides a platform for theologizing in

8.8 All-out celebration in Benin.

context. The word becomes incarnated within the soils of Africa through her peoples and music.

Let All People Sing His Praise

Finally, the African church soundscape is ringing more and more with the praises of God in culturally appropriate and meaningful ways. The dynamic vitality of the church is expressed in the new voice of her songs, songs that interact dynamically with one another in community in the presence of the triune God. More and more African Christian music is becoming global and also contributing to the church worldwide.

How should the church embrace its global reality in terms of music? How is the reign of God given priority in all situations? A dynamic tension and balance between life's realities and the movement of God must be maintained. We are well advised to take Eugene Petersen's wise counsel to heart as he reminds us that:

> We need to know the creation-reality in which we are placed. But we also have to cultivate a fear-of-the-Lord appropriate and adequate to this reality. We need to live in a way that is congruent with where we are. (2005, 108)

The church in sub-Saharan Africa has begun the process of singing and making music in ways that are congruent with where they are. It is a process that requires continual renewal just as does the global church. The reality is that there is one God and many voices; there are many musical expressions, languages of praise, and adoration in which the ultimate intention is to point to the glory of God in our lives. Just as the song in Revelation says, the peoples are coming "from every tribe and language and people and nations"; they have come into the kingdom and been made priests to serve Him (Rev 5:9b—10a). May the church around the world sing new songs that make Jesus Christ known throughout the whole earth.

For Discussion

1. Share stories of musical ethnocentrism you have experienced at home, among your friends, and in the church. How do you feel when someone condemns the music that is special to you? What suggestions do you have for overcoming musical ethnocentrism?

2. What are biblical patterns for using music in the church in ways that make the Good News understandable within any culture?

3. Sing or listen to five contrasting Christian songs. After each song, share in groups what the songs mean to each person. Note the different meanings that arise within your small group.

4. What are the streams of music present within your church tradition? What is being done to embrace, recognize, and incorporate each one within your church in ways that recognize the diversity of your congregation?

5. Identify and discuss the main approaches to music in the life of the African church that can contribute to music in the church around the world?

6. CLASS PROJECT: Design and create a contextualized worship service for a local context, that is, a specific group of people. This may be for Africa, Asia, Latin America, or a group of people in Europe or North America. The local context may be cross-cultural, cross-generational, or one that the church has not addressed.

Follow these steps:

1. Identify the musical streams already present within that context.

2. Design the service based on the goals of

   a. using music for building the faith of Christian believers,

   b. respecting each group of people in the selected people group by drawing from their musical heritage and styles, and

   c. creating Christian community by composing new songs that are congruent with our time and local context.

3. Incorporate at least one to two new songs that are culturally appropriate to the group selected.

4. Present the worship service.

5. Afterward, evaluate it according to the three goals and analyze it according to figure 8.1.

6. Then create a plan for implementing this approach in your local church or mission outreach.

Appendix
Electronic Resources

The Internet is rich with resources on music in the African Church and African music. This appendix is a beginning list of the some of the most important Web sites currently available. There are three parts to this list of references: music in the African Church, African music, and general Web sites where you can find additional resources about Africa and Christianity in Africa. Many of these sites make the purchase of CDs and DVDs of both African and African church music available as well.

MUSIC IN THE AFRICAN CHURCH

Africa, International Council of EthnoDoxologists available at www. worldofworship.org/search/index.php?zoom_query=Africa.

Agordoh, A. A. "The Present State of Church Music in Ghana." In *Institute of African Studies: Research Review* available at www. ajol.info/viewarticle.php?jid=133&id=13560&layout=abstract.

Barz, Gregory. *Kwayas: "They're Singing Jazz in the Church!"* available at http://research.umbc.edu/efhm/2/barz/barz2.html.

Creary, Nicholas M. *African Inculturation of the Catholic Church in Zimbabwe, 1858–1977* available at www.encyclopedia.com/doc/1G1-56909069.html.

God Hears My Song: Worship Music from the Cameroon (CD) available at http://lbt.gospelcom.net/stories/07-1/godhears.htm.

King, Roberta R. *Resources in African Christian Music* available at www.fuller.edu/sis/conc/gcw.asp.

Morley, Steve. *Soweto Gospel Choir: African Spirit Transcript* available at www.umc.org/site/c.lwL4KnN1LtH/b.2629021/k.6992/ Soweto_Gospel_Choir_iAfrican_Spiriti.htm.

Parsitau, Damaris Seleina. *"Then Sings My Soul": Gospel Music as Popular Culture in the Spiritual Lives of Kenyan Pentecostal/Charismatic Christians* available at www.usask.ca/relst/jrpc/art14-singsmysoul.html.

Quinn, Richard J. *African Video Collections—Harvard College Library* available at http://hcl.harvard.edu/research/guides/africa/videos/a-c.html.

Thompson, Jack. "Donald Fraser and the Ngoni Church." In *The Occasion of the Centenary of Loudon Station* available at http://embangweni.com/FraserNgoni.htm.

The Traditional Music and Cultures of Kenya available at www.blue-gecko.org/kenya/index.htm.

African Music

Africa, Music Library, and Listening Center: The University of Washington Libraries available at www.lib.washington.edu/music/world.html#africa.

Africa on Rootsworld available at www.rootsworld.com/africa/.

The African Music Encyclopedia available at http://africanmusic.org/.

African Music on the Internet available at www-sul.stanford.edu/africa/music.html.

African Music Section: The Society for Ethnomusicology available at www.yorku.ca/africsem/africanmusiclinks.htm.

African Musical Instruments available at www.kalimba.co.za/index.html.

African Popular Music 1931–1957 available at http://pages.unibas.ch/africanmusic/archives/index.htm.

Afrique: Collection Ethnomad (Ateliers d'ethnomusicology) available at www.adem.ch/CD/cdafrique.html.

Balafon available at www.masabo.com/balafon.html.

calabash music: tune your world available at http://music.calabash-music.com/world/africa.

Cherry, Eric. *African Music Links: West African Music* available at http://echarry.web.wesleyan.edu/Afmus.html.

Cora Connection available at www.coraconnection.com/.

International Library of African Music available at http://ilam.ru.ac.
za/amj.php.

Music and Dance of Africa, Columbia University Libraries available at www.columbia.edu/cu/lweb/indiv/africa/cuvl/music.
html#marimbalafon.

The Music of Africa: Breadth and diversity available at http://world-
views.igc.org/awpguide/music.html.

University of California Los Angeles Ethnomusicology Archive, Field
Recordings, West Africa available at www.ethnomusic.ucla.edu/
archive/collafricawest.htm.

AFRICA AND AFRICAN CHRISTIANITY

Africa South of the Sahara available at www.sul.stanford.edu/africa/
guide3.html.

African Christianity: A History of the Christian Church in Africa available at www.bethel.edu/~letnie/AfricanChristianity/SSARCCs-
inceVaticanII.html.

BBC World Service: The Story of Africa: African Churches available
at www.bbc.co.uk/worldservice/specials/1624_story_of_africa/
page73.shtml.

Christianity in Africa available at www-sul.stanford.edu/africa/reli-
gion/christianity-in-africa.html.

Notes

CHAPTER ONE

1. Annetta Miller, *Sharing Boundaries: Learning the Wisdom of Africa* (Nairobi: Pauline Publications Africa, 2003), 76.
2. *Côte d'Ivoire* is what was formerly called the Ivory Coast.
3. See David B. Barrett, Alan W. Eister, Cuthbert K. Omari, and John S. Mbiti, *African Initiatives in Religion: 21 Studies from Eastern and Central Africa* (Nairobi: East African Publishing House, 1971).
4. Alan P. Merriam, *The Anthropology of Music* (Evanston Ill: Northwestern University Press, 1964). Ethnomusicology is the study of music and its relationship to culture. Scholars continue to study music in its cultural context, music *in* culture, and music *as* culture. Bruno Nettl, *The Study of Ethnomusicology: Thirty-one Issues and Concepts*, 2nd ed. (Urbana: University of Illinois Press, 2005), 215–31. The emergent discipline offers approaches for understanding the link between music and culture.
5. Missiology includes studies in biblical theology, intercultural studies, ecclesiology, and spiritual pilgrimage.
6. Karl Barth. *Church Dogmatics*, translated by G. W. Bromiley, edited by G. W. Bromiley and T. F. Torrance, 2nd ed., vol. I/1 (Edinburgh: T&T Clark, 1975). Barth considered dogmatics the most important approach to theology as the Church's distinctive talk about God: "As a theological discipline dogmatics is the scientific self-examination of the Christian Church with respect to the content of its distinctive talk about God" (I/1:3).

7. http://www.worldchristiandatabase.org/wcd/esweb. asp?WCI=Results&Query=415. The *World Christian Database* accessed on June 22, 2007 reported 422,797,295 Christians on the African continent. The *World Christian Database* incorporates the core data with significant updates from the *World Christian Encyclopedia*. David B. Barrett, Todd M. Johnson, and George T. Kurian, *World Christian Encyclopedia* (New York: Oxford University Press, 2001).
8. Kwame Anthony Appiah and Henry Louis Gates Jr., eds., *"Languages, African: An Overview,"* in *Africana: The Encyclopedia of the African and African American Experience* (Oxford; New York: Oxford University Press, 2005), 3:510. At least twenty-nine African languages have a minimum of 1 million speakers, and this ranges up to 160 million Arabic speakers. Note that distinct African languages are so numerous that the average number of people speaking any one African language is 200,000.

CHAPTER TWO

1. Miller, *Sharing Boundaries*, 22.
2. *Balafon* is the common term for a wood-frame xylophone in West Africa, which literally means "the wood that speaks." It is called a *jegele* in the Cebaara-Senufo language.
3. Exceptions to this norm are found among the African Instituted Churches that arose either in reaction to the Euro-American worship traditions imposed on them or where the gospel was presented in local, indigenous African formats. This is discussed in greater detail in chapter 3.
4. Ian Bradley, *Abide with Me: The World of Victorian Hymns* (Chicago: GIA Publications, 1997), 5. Barrel organs were in essence pipe organs operated by a barrel mechanism that played a standardized repertoire of twenty or more metrical psalms.
5. The American Sunday School Union was patterned after the London Sunday School Union, that was formed in 1803.

CHAPTER THREE

1. Joseph G. Healey, *Once upon a Time in Africa: Stories of Wisdom and Joy* (Maryknoll, N.Y.: Orbis Books, 2004), 85.
2. Case studies include John Blacking, *Venda Children's Songs: A Study in Ethnomusicological Analysis* (Johannesburg, Witwatersrand University Press, 1967). J. H. Kwabena Nketia, *The Music of Africa* (New York: W. W. Norton, 1974) is a well-known cumulative approach.
3. See G. P. Murdock, *Africa: Its Peoples and their Culture History* (New York: McGraw-Hill, 1959); and J. H. Greenberg, *The Languages of Africa* (Bloomington: Indiana University Press, 1966).

4. For instrument classification system, see Klaus P. Wachsmann, Erich M. von Honbostel, and Curt Sachs, "Instruments, Classification of," in the *New Grove Dictionary of Music and Musicians* (London: Macmillan Press, 1980) 9:237–45.
5. Much of this information is garnered from Nketia, *The Music of Africa* and Alfred L. Kroeber, "The Cultural Area and Age Area Concepts of Clark Wissler," in *Methods in Social Science*, ed. Stuart A. Rice (Chicago: University of Chicago Press, 1931), 248–65.
6. Colin Turnbull, *The Forest People* (New York: Simon & Schuster, 1968). This classic study of the Mbuti who lived in the rainforest in Congo demonstrated that they had no drums. Michelle Robin Kisliuk, *Seize the Dance!: BaAka Musical Life and the Ethnography of Performance* (New York: Oxford University Press, 1998). This study of the BaAka confirmed this stereotype of forest nomads.
7. In *The Music of Africa*, Nketia discusses the function of music in society, vocal and choral ensembles, instrument types, and their distribution across Africa. In *The Anthropology of Music*, Merriam recognized the importance of song texts as a basis for understanding human behavior. Eileen Southern, *The Music of Black Americans* (New York: W. W. Norton, 1971). Southern characterizes these traits as the fundamental African musical legacy in the Americas.
8. Personal research 2001.
9. Gunther Wagner, *The Bantu of Western Kenya: With Special Reference to the Vugusu and Logoli* (London: Oxford University Press, 1949/70).
10. One song adopted nationally in Kenya from the Abaluyia of Western Kenya is *Mwana Mberi*, a song decrying the pain of the first time a woman gives birth, which is sung at all three occasions to celebrate the beginning and end of life, the strength displayed the first time an opponent is floored—whether in wrestling matches or at a political rally.
11. See discussions by musicians, scholars, and missionaries in early editions of the *Journal of African Music* on the merits and demerits of African music for Christian worship. See also Ruth Stone, ed., *The Garland Handbook of African Music*, vol. 1 (New York, Garland Publishing, 2000).
12. Lester Monts, "Islam in Liberia," in *Garland Encyclopedia of World Music*, vol. 1, ed. Ruth Stone (New York: Garland Publishers, 1998), 327–49. Monts discusses the kinds of changes in music as different brands of Islam were adopted in Liberia.
13. Nketia, *The Music of Africa*, 21–50. Nketia discusses music in community life including how individuals and groups reinforced their musical and social identity through participation, observation, and training relative to each group's requirement. The grouping might be relative to language, class, gender, and occupation.

14. Blacking, *Venda Children's Songs*, reinforces this view.
15. See Kofi Agawu, *Representing African Music: Postcolonial Notes, Queries, Positions* (London: Routledge, 2003) for a discussion of some of the effects.

CHAPTER FOUR

1. *"Ka slu dimesh ndo bai; ka gotso ngece ndo bai,"* source and translation by Rev. Dr. Moussa Bongoyok.
2. Bruno Nettl, "The Fourth Age," in *The Western Impact on World Music* (New York: Schirmer Books, 1985), 3–6.
3. Jean Suret-Canale, *Afrique Noire: L'ère coloniale, 1900–1945* (Paris: Editions sociales, 1977).
4. Quoted in Philippe Oberlé, *Côte d'Ivoire: Images du passé, 1888–1980* (Colmar, France: S.A.E.P., 1986), 62.
5. David Dargie, "Christian Music among Africans," in *Christianity in South Africa*, ed. Richard Elphick and Rodney Davenport (Berkeley: University of California Press, 1997), 321.
6. In *What Western Christians Can Learn from African-Initiated Churches*, Mission Insight series, no. 10, ed. James R. Krabill (Elkhart, Ind.: Mennonite Board of Missions, 2000), 1.
7. Three among many of the works describing the multifaceted nature of these movements are: Allan Anderson, *African Reformation: African Initiated Christianity in the 20th Century* (Trenton, N.J. and Asmara, Eritrea: Africa World Press, 2001); David B. Barrett, *Schism and Renewal in Africa* (Nairobi, Addis Ababa, Lusaka: Oxford Press, 1968); and Inus Daneel, *Quest for Belonging* (Harare: Mambo Press, 1987).
8. Harold W. Turner. *African Independent Church*, vol. 2 (Oxford: Clarendon, 1967). Turner referred to these movements as "neo-primal," "synthetist," "hebraist," "independent churches," and "mission-founded churches." I will retain some of his terms, modify others, and add one more to reflect certain current realities that did not exist at the time of his research. To examine more closely some of Turner's early attempts to sketch out this typology, see Harold W. Turner, "Classification and Nomenclature of Modern African Religious Groups," in *African Independent Church Movements*, edited by V. E. W. Hayward (London: Edinburgh House Press, 1963), 13; and Turner, "A Typology for African Religious Movements," *Journal of Religion in Africa* 1 (1967): 18–21; "A Typology of Modern African Religious Movements," Journal of Religion and Religions 1 (1967): 1–34.
9. See Bengt Gustaf Malcolm Sundkler, *Bantu Prophets in South Africa* (London: Lutterworth Press, 1961; 1st ed., 1948), 193 for the Zulu Zionists; J. Akinyele Omoyajowo, *Cherubim and Seraphim: The History of the African Independent Church* (New York: NOK Publishers Interna-

tional, 1982), 159 for the Cherubim and Seraphim; and Turner, *African Independent Church* 2:296 for the Church of the Lord (Aladura).

10. Ruth Ellenberger, "Gossiping the Gospel in French West Africa," *The Alliance Weekly*, September 13, 1930, 598.

11. See W. J. Wallace, "Hymns in Ethiopia," *Practical Anthropology* 9 (1962): 271; and Mary Key, "Hymn Writing with Indigenous Tunes," *Practical Anthropology* 9 (1962): 258–62.

12. This statement is from the third international consultation of the Lutheran World Federation's Study Team on Worship and Culture held in Nairobi, Kenya, in January 1996. Cf. Website www.worship.ca

13. Quoted in Bruce Britten, *We Don't Want Your White Religion* (Manzini, Swaziland, 1984), 26.

14. Ephraim Amu, *Amu Choral Works*, vol. 1 (Accra, Ghana: Waterville Publishing House, 1993), 8. These comments are from J. H. Kwabena Nketia in the introduction.

CHAPTER FIVE

1. Translated from the *Akan* language by Thomas Oduro.
2. Ethnographic diary and notes of Jean Kidula from her father's funeral.
3. Also commonly referred to as African Instituted Churches.

CHAPTER SIX

1. Translated from the *Akan* language by Thomas Oduro.
2. Many of the observations in this chapter are from the author's research and experience in Anglophone East, South, and West Africa, and in Francophone Central Africa, and in Ethiopia, Sudan, and Côte d'Ivoire. Anglophone countries were those originally or eventually colonized by the British. France or Belgium's colonies are Francophone.
3. Agawu, *Representing African Music*, 20. Agawu notes that "the most profound aspect of the impact of colonialism . . . [was] the transformation in terms of discourse about African music. . . ." This discourse translates into imagined and real presentations and representations of African music, or music by Africans, that have been frozen and stereotyped in commercial and academic media.
4. Chinua Achebe, *Things Fall Apart* (London: Heinemann, 1958); and James Ngugi wa Thiong'o, *The River Between* (London, Heinemann, 1956). These two novels fictionalize the realities of these tensions.
5. Rev. Brother Basil, "The Dilemna of Bantu Church Music," *African Music* 1, no. 4 (1957): 36–39; Lazarus M. Ekueme, "African Music in Christian Liturgy, the Igbo Experiment," *African Music* 5, no. 3 (1971): 12–33; Robert A. Kauffman, "Impressions of African Church Music," *African Music* 3, no. 3 (1964): 109–10; Joseph Lenherr "Advancing Indigenous Church Music" *African Music* 4, no. 2 (1968): 33–39;

Canon E. E. Lury, "Music in East African Churches," *African Music* 1, no. 3 (1956): 34–36. Discussions of music used by different Christian denominations in Africa are prevalent in these and other articles of the journal *African Music* dating from 1954 to 1976.

6. Nketia, *The Music of Africa*. This text provides numerous examples of music as a social event: pure entertainment, verbal communication of values and beliefs, to articulate and resolve communal concerns, in rites of passage, and to promote social identity and cohesion.

7. Agawu, *Representing African Music*, 8–15. Agawu discusses the introduction of formal music education in Ghana and the role of the church in introducing European tonalities and harmonies. Similar behaviors were introduced in other African countries.

8. Christopher Small, *Musicking* (Middleton, Conn.: Wesleyan University Press, 1998). Small coined the term *musicking*, and it has gained wide acceptance as definitive of music not just as a product (a noun) but also a process (a verb). Its employment embraces the concept and definition of music beyond Eurocentric parameters of sound—to sounding, visuals and seeing, motor, and feeling.

9. Anglophone Africa and Francophone Central Africa embraced the choral phenomenon. Francophone West Africa and some of Sudanic Africa are beginning to develop such groups.

10. Clara Henderson and Lisa Gilman, "Women as Religious and Political Praise Singers within African Institutions: The Case of the CCAP Blantyre Synod and Political Parties in Malawi," *Women and Music: A Journal of Gender and Culture* 8 (2004): 22–40. This article is a good example of the intersection of religion, politics, and gender in the formation of choral groups in Malawi.

11. Footnote 5 suggests sources for this information

12. See Abamfo Atiemo, "Singing with Understanding: A Study of Gospel Music in Ghana," *Studies in World Christianity* 12, no. 2 (2006): 142–63; Ezra Chitando, *Singing Culture: A Study of Gospel Music in Zimbabwe* (Uppsala, Sweden: Nordiska Africainstitutet, 2002); and Jean Kidula, "'Sing and Shine': Religious Popular Music in Kenya," Ph.D. diss., University of California, Los Angeles, 1998.

CHAPTER SEVEN

1. (*Qui cantat, bis orat*) literally "he who sings, prays twice"—Augustine of Hippo *Sermons 336*, 1 PL 38, 1472.

2. F. B. Welbourn and B. A. Ogot, *A Place to Feel at Home: A Study of Two Independent Churches in Western Kenya* (London: Oxford University Press, 1966).

3. Welbourn and Ogot, *A Place to Feel at Home*. The Church of Christ in Africa came out of the Anglican work of the Church Missionary Soci-

ety in Western Kenya and the African Israel Church Nineveh stemmed from Pentecostal Missions.

4. Roberta R. King, *A Time to Sing: A Manual for the African Church* (Nairobi: Evangel Publishing House, 1999), 57–78. King describes a treatment of differing call-and-response forms.

5. James R. Krabill, *The Hymnody of the Harrist Church among the Dida of South-Central Ivory Coast (1913–1949)*, vol. 74 (Frankfurt am Main: Peter Lang, 1995), 379–81. Krabill discusses a theological development of moving "From Law to Spirit," one of the most distinctive features of the Prophet Harris's teaching.

6. See John S. Mbiti, "Some African Concepts of Christology," in *Christ and the Younger Churches*, edited by G. F. Vicedom, 51–62 (London: SPCK, 1972); and John V. Taylor, *The Primal Vision: Christian Presence amid African Religion* (London: SCM Press, 1963).

7. *Ayi wowo*: a musical vocable, both a composition technique and a textual means of strengthening the element of surprise.

8. The Senufo expression for becoming a Christian and also worshiping God in daily living.

9. During my research on Senufo Christian songs in the 1980s, findings led to a theory of creative contextualization, that is, the use of culturally appropriate songs makes a difference in the growth and development of the church.

10. King, *A Time to Sing*. King offers help with composing in groups.

11. From personal field notes based on a training course in 1993 at Daystar University in Nairobi, Kenya.

CHAPTER EIGHT

1. Miller, *Sharing Boundaries*, 108.
2. Personal research in Kenya, circa 1992.
3. *Uhuru* is Kiswahili for independence—such as in post-independent Africa when colonization was withdrawn.
4. A Kenyan Kiswahili chorus style.
5. King, *A Time to Sing*. King's work develops this methodology.

Bibliography

Achebe, Chinua. 1958. *Things Fall Apart*. London: Heinemann.

Agawu, Kofi. 2003. *Representing African Music: Postcolonial Notes, Queries, Positions*. London: Routledge.

Amu, Ephraim. 1993. *Amu Choral Works*. Vol. 1. Accra, Ghana: Waterville Publishing House.

Anderson, Allan. 2001. *African Reformation: African Initiated Christianity in the 20th Century*. Trenton, N.J. and Asmara, Eritrea: Africa World Press.

Appiah, Kwame Anthony, and Henry Louis Gates Jr., eds. 2005. "Languages, African: An Overview." In *Africana: The Encyclopedia of the African and African American Experience*, 3:510–12. Oxford; New York: Oxford University Press.

Askew, Kelly Michelle. 2002. *Performing the Nation: Swahili Music and Cultural Politics in Tanzania*. Chicago: University of Chicago Press.

Atiemo, Abamfo. 2006. "Singing with Understanding: A Study of Gospel Music in Ghana." *Studies in World Christianity* 12 (2):142–63.

Barrett, David B. 1968. *Schism and Renewal in Africa*. Nairobi: Oxford Press.

Barrett, David B., Alan W. Eister, Cuthbert K. Omari, and John S. Mbiti. 1971. *African Initiatives in Religion: 21 Studies from Eastern and Central Africa*. Nairobi: East African Publishing House.

Barrett, David B., Todd M. Johnson, and George T. Kurian. 2001.

World Christian Encyclopedia. 2nd ed. Vol. 1. New York: Oxford University Press.

Barth, Karl. 1975. *Church Dogmatics.* Translated by G. W. Bromiley. Edited by G. W. Bromiley and T. F. Torrance. 2nd ed. Vol. I/1. Edinburgh: T&T Clark.

Basil, Brother. 1957. "The Dilemna of Bantu Church Music." *African Music* 1(4): 36–39.

Baur, John. 1998. *2000 Years of Christianity in Africa.* Nairobi: Paulines Publications Africa.

Berliner, Paul. 1981. *The Soul of Mbira: Music and Traditions of the Shona People of Zimbabwe.* Berkeley: University of California Press.

Blacking, John. 1967. *Venda Children's Songs: A Study in Ethnomusicological Analysis.* Johannesburg: Witwatersrand University Press.

Bradley, Ian. 1997. *Abide With Me: The World of Victorian Hymns.* Chicago: GIA Publications.

Britten, Bruce. 1984. *We Don't Want Your White Religion.* Manzini, Swaziland.

Campbell, Karen. 2003. "How Can We Sing Songs in a Strange Land." Paper presented at Global Consultation on Music and Mission, Fort Worth, Texas.

Chenoweth, Vida, and Darlene Bee. 1968. "On Ethnic Music." *Practical Anthropology* 15: 205–12.

Chitando, Ezra. 2002. *Singing Culture: A Study of Gospel Music in Zimbabwe.* Uppsala, Sweden: Nordiska Africainstitutet.

Corbitt, J. Nathan. 1994. "Dynamism in African Church Music: The Search for Identity and Self Expression." *Black Sacred Music: A Journal of Theomusicology* 8(2): 1–29.

———. 2002. "Christian Music in Africa." *EthnoDoxology* 1(2): 1–6.

Daneel, Inus. 1987. *Quest for Belonging.* Harare, Zimbabwe: Mambo Press.

Dargie, David. 1997. "Christian Music among Africans." In *Christianity in South Africa.* Edited by Richard Elphick and Rodney Davenport, 319–26. Berkeley: University of California Press.

Darkwa, Asante. 1980. "New Horizons in Music and Worship in Ghana." *African Urban Studies* [African Studies Center, Michigan State University] 8: 63–70.

De Surgy, Albert. 2001a. *L'Église du Christianisme Céleste: Un exemple d'Église prophétique au Bénin.* Paris: Editions Karthala.

————. 2001b. *Le phénomène pentecôtiste en Afrique noire: Le cas béninois*. Paris: L'Harmattan.

Dickson, Andrew William. 1992. *The Story of Christian Music*. Oxford: Lion Publishing.

Ekueme, Lazarus M. 1971. "African Music in Christian Liturgy, the Igbo Experiment." *African Music* 5(3): 12–33.

Ellenberger, Ruth. "Gossiping the Gospel in French West Africa." *The Alliance Weekly*, September 13, 1930, 596, 598.

Esker, Harry, and Hugh McElrath. 1995. *Sing with Understanding*, 2nd ed. Nashville: Church Street Press.

Fasholé-Luke, Edward, Richard Gray, Adrian Hastings, and Godwin Tasie, eds. 1978. *Christianity in Independent Africa*. Bloomington: Indiana University Press.

Friedson, Steven M. 1996. *Dancing Prophets: Musical Experience in Tumbuka Healing*. Chicago: University of Chicago Press.

Gifford, Paul. 1993. *Christianity and Politics in Doe's Liberia*. Cambridge: Cambridge University Press.

Greenberg, J. H. 1966. *The Languages of Africa*. Bloomington: Indiana University Press.

Grenz, Stanley. 1993. *Revisioning Evangelical Theology: A Fresh Agenda for the 21st Century*. Downers Grove: InterVarsity.

Hastings, Adrian. 1976. *African Christianity*. New York: The Seabury Press.

————. 1994. *The Church in Africa: 1450–1950*. Oxford: Clarendon.

Hayward, V. E. W., ed. 1963, *African Independent Church Movements*. London: Edinburgh House Press.

Healey, Joseph G. 2004. *Once Upon a Time in Africa: Stories of Wisdom and Joy*. Maryknoll, NY: Orbis Books.

Henderson, Clara, and Lisa Gilman. 2004 "Women as Religious and Political Praise Singers within African Institutions: The Case of the CCAP Blantyre Synod and Political Parties in Malawi." *Women and Music: A Journal of Gender and Culture* 8: 22–40.

Hiebert, Paul G. 1985. *Anthropological Insights for Missionaries*. Grand Rapids: Baker Book House.

Hollenweger, Walter. 1977. *The Pentecostals*. Minneapolis: Augsburg Publishing House.

Hustad, Donald P. 1993. *Jubilate II: Church Music in Worship and Renewal*. Carol Stream, Ill.: Hope Publishing.

Idowu, E. Bolaji. 1965. *Towards an Indigenous Church*. London: Oxford University Press.

Isichei, Elizabeth. 1995. *A History of Christianity in Africa*. Grand Rapids: Eerdmans.

Jacob, W. M. 2006. Editorial. *Theology* 109 (848): 81–82.

Jenkins, Philip. 2002. *The Next Christendom: The Coming of Global Christianity*. Oxford: Oxford University Press.

Jones, A. M. 1976. *African Hymnody in Christian Worship: A Contribution to the History of Its Development*. Gwelo, Rhodesia: Mambo Press.

Kasiera, Ezekiel. 1981. "The Development of Pentecostal Christianity in Western Kenya: With Special Reference to Maragoli, Nyang'ori and Tiriki 1909–1942." Ph.D. diss., University of Aberdeen.

Kauffman, Robert A. 1964. "Impressions of African Church Music." *African Music* 3(3): 109–10.

Keller, Marian. n.d. *Twenty Years in Africa, 1913–1933: Retrospect and Prospect*. Toronto: Full Gospel Publishing.

Key, Mary. 1962. "Hymn Writing with Indigenous Tunes." *Practical Anthropology* 9: 258–62.

Kidula, Jean Ngoya. 1998. "'Sing and Shine': Religious Popular Music in Kenya." Ph.D. diss., University of California, Los Angeles.

———. 2000. "Polishing the Luster of the Stars: Professionalism made Workable in Kenya." *Ethnomusicology* 44 no. 3: 408–28.

———. 2005. "Christian Music as Indigenous African: Appropriation and Accommodation." In *Multiple Interpretations of Dynamics and Knowledge in African Music Traditions: A Festschrift in Honor of Akin Euba*. Edited by George Dor and Bode Omojola, 211–26. Point Richmond, Calif.: Music Research Institute Press.

King, Roberta R. 1989. "Pathways in Christian Music Communication: The Case of the Senufo of Cote d'Ivoire." Ph.D. diss., Fuller Theological Seminary.

———. 1999a. *A Time to Sing: A Manual for the African Church*. Nairobi: Evangel Publishing House.

———. 1999b. *Ethnomusicology*. In *Evangelical Dictionary of World Missions*. Edited by A. S. Moreau, 327–28. Grand Rapids: Baker Books.

———. 2004. "Toward a Discipline of Christian Ethnomusicology: A Missiological Paradigm." *Missiology: An International Review* 32(3): 293–307.

Kisliuk, Michelle Robin. 1998. *Seize the Dance!: BaAka Musical Life and the Ethnography of Performance*. New York: Oxford University Press.

Krabill, James R. 1995. *The Hymnody of the Harrist Church among the Dida of South-Central Ivory Coast (1913–1949)*, vol. 74. Frankfurt am Main: Peter Lang.

———. 2006. "Theology of Song." In *Global Consultation on Music and Missions: The Proceedings*. Edited by Paul Neeley, Linda Neeley, Paul McAndrew, and Cathy McAndrew. Duncanville, Tex: Ethnodoxology/ACT.

Kraft, Charles H. 1991. *Communication Theory for Christian Witness*. Rev. ed. Maryknoll, N.Y.: Orbis Books.

Kroeber, Alfred L. 1931. "The Cultural Area and Age Area Concepts of Clark Wissler." In *Methods in Social Science*. Edited by Stuart A. Rice, 248–65. Chicago: University of Chicago Press.

Larbi, Kingsley. 2001. *Pentecostalism: The Eddies of Ghanaian Christianity*. Accra, Ghana: Blessed Publications.

Lenherr, J. 1968. "Advancing Indigenous Church Music." *African Music* 4(2): 33–39.

Levine, Laurie. 2005. *The Traditional Music of South Africa*. Johannesburg: Jacana.

Lury, E. E. 1956. "Music in East African Churches." *African Music* 1(3): 34–36.

Lutheran World Federation's Study Team on Worship and Culture. 1996. "Culture Statement." www.worship.ca.

Makhubu, Paul. 1988. *Who are the Independent Churches?* Johannesburg: Skotaville Publishers.

Marini, Stephen A., ed. 2006. "Hymnody and History: Early American Evangelical Hymns as Sacred Music." In *Music in American Religious Experience*. Edited by P. V. Bohlman, Edith L. Blumhofer and Maria M. Chow, 123–54. New York: Oxford University Press.

Masa, Bongaye Senza. 1975. "The Future of African Music." In *African Challenge*. Chap. 14. Edited by Kenneth Y. Best, 146–59. Nairobi: Transafrica Publishers.

Mbiti, John S. 1970. *African Religions and Philosophy*. Garden City, N.Y.: Doubleday.

———. 1972. "Some African Concepts of Christology." In *Christ and the Younger Churches*. Edited by G. F. Vicedom. London: SPCK.

———. 1975. *Introduction to African Religion*. Nairobi: Heinemann.

Mbunga, Stephen B. G. 1963. "Church Law and Bantu Music: Ecclesiastical Documents and Law on Sacred Music as Applied to Bantu Music." *Neue Zeitschrift fuer Missionswissenschaft*, Suppl. 13, 1964, vol. 20, 231–32.

———. 1968. "African Church Music." *African Ecclesiastical Review* 10: 372–77.

McCall, John. 1998. "The Representation of African Music in Early Documents." In *Africa* of *Garland Encyclopedia of World Music*, vol. 1. Edited by Ruth Stone, 74–100. New York: Garland Publishers.

Merriam, Alan P. 1964. *The Anthropology of Music*. Evanston Ill.: Northwestern University Press.

Middleton, John, ed. 1997. "Language Classification." In *Encyclopedia of Africa South of the Sahara*, 2: 796–99. New York: Charles Scribner's Sons.

Miller, Annetta. 2003. *Sharing Boundaries: Learning the Wisdom of Africa*. Nairobi: Pauline Publications Africa.

Monts, Lester. 1998. "Islam in Liberia." In *Africa* of *Garland Encyclopedia of World Music*, vol. 1. Edited by Ruth Stone, 327–49. New York: Garland Publishers.

Morehouse, Katherine. 2006. "The Western Hymn in Mission: Intrusion or Tradition?" In *Global Consultation on Music and Missions: The Proceedings*. Edited by Paul Neeley, Linda Neeley, Paul McAndrew, and Cathy McAndrew. Duncanville, Tex.: Ethnodoxology/ACT.

Morse, Laverne R. 1975. "Ethnomusicology: A New Frontier." *Evangelical Missions Quarterly* 11: 32–37.

Moury, de S. G. Mgr., and T. R. P. Chabert. 1922. "Jubilé sacerdotal." *Echo des missions africaines* (September): 133–34 and (October): 149.

Murdock, G. P. 1959. *Africa: Its People, and Their Culture History*. New York: McGraw-Hill.

Murray, Francis. 1966. "Adaptation and the 1968 Missal." *African Ecclesial Review* 8: 317–22.

Musicae Sacrae Disciplina. 1955. Papal Encyclical. Herder Korrespondenz.

Musumba, Florence 'Ngale. 1993. "Effects of Acculturation on Church Music: A Case Study of the Church of God in East Africa—(Nairobi)." M.A. thesis, Kenyatta University, Nairobi, Kenya.

"Nairobi Statement on Worship and Culture." 1996. From the third international consultation of the Lutheran World Federation's Study Team on Worship and Culture, held in Nairobi, Kenya, in January. http://www.worship.ca.

Nancy, Hardy. 1993. "The Worshipping Church in Africa." *A Journal of Theo-musicology in Black Sacred Music* 7(2): 4–59.

Nettl, Bruno. 2005. *The Study of Ethnomusicology: Thirty-one Issues and Concepts*. 2nd ed. Urbana: University of Illinois Press.

———. 1985. "The Fourth Age." In *The Western Impact on World Music: Change, Adaptation, and Survival*, 3–6. New York: Schirmer Books.

Nketia, J. H. Kwabena. 1958. "The Contribution of African Culture to Christian Worship." *International Review of Missions* 47: 265–278.

———. 1974. *The Music of Africa*. New York: W.W. Norton.

———. 1986. "Perspectives on African Musicology." In *Africa and the West*. Edited by Isaac James Mowoe and Richard Bjornson, 215–53. Westport, Conn.: Greenwood Press.

Oberlé, Philippe. 1986. *Côte d'Ivoire: Images du passé, 1888–1980*. Colmar, France: S.A.E.P.

Olupona, Jacob, ed. 2000. *African Spirituality: Forms, Meanings and Expressions*. New York: Crossroad Publishing.

Omoyajowo, J. Akinyele. 1982. *Cherubim and Seraphim: The History of the African Independent Church*. New York: NOK Publishers International.

Opoku, Kofi Asare. 1978. *West African Traditional Religion*. Accra, Ghana: FEP International.

p'Bitek, Okot. 1973. *Africa's Cultural Revolution*. Nairobi: Macmillan Books for Africa.

Peterson, Eugene H. 2005. *Christ Plays in Ten Thousand Places: A Conversation in Spiritual Theology*. Grand Rapids: Eerdmans.

Pobee, Joseph S., and Gabriel Ositelu II. 1998. *African Initiatives in Christianity*. Geneva: WCC Publications.

Sanneh, Lamin. 1983. *West African Christianity: The Religious Impact*. Maryknoll, N.Y.: Orbis Books.

Shank, David A. *What Western Christians Can Learn from African-Initiated Churches*. Mission Insight ser. no. 10. Edited by James R. Krabill. Elkhart, Ind.: Mennonite Board of Missions, 2000.

Shaw, Mark. 2000. "Africa." In *Evangelical Dictionary of World Missions*. Edited by A. S. Moreau, 37–42. Grand Rapids: Baker Books.

Shenk, Wilbert R. 1999. *Changing Frontiers of Mission*. Maryknoll, N.Y.: Orbis Books.

Small, Christopher. 1998. *Musicking*. Middleton, Conn.: Wesleyan University Press.

Smith, Donald K. 1992. *Creating Understanding: A Handbook for Christian Communication across Cultural Landscapes*. Grand Rapids: Zondervan

Southern, Eileen. 1971. *The Music of Black Americans*. New York: W.W. Norton.

Stapleton, Chris, and Chris May. 1987. *Africa All-Stars: The Pop Music of a Continent*. London: Paladin.

Stevenson, W. R. 1892. "Foreign Missions." In *A Dictionary of Hymnology: Setting Forth the Origin and History of Christian Hymns of All Ages and Nations*. Edited by John Julian, 738–59. London: John Murray.

Stinton, Diane B. 2004. *Jesus of Africa: Voices of Contemporary African Christology*. Maryknoll, N.Y.: Orbis Books.

Stone, Ruth. 1998a. "African Music in a Constellation of Arts." In *The Garland Encyclopedia of World Music*, vol 1. Edited by Ruth Stone, 7–12. New York and London: Garland Publishing.

———, ed. 1998b. *Garland Encyclopedia of World Music*, vol. 1:*Africa*. New York and London: Garland Publishing.

———, ed. 2000. *The Garland Handbook of African Music*. New York: Garland Publishing.

Stowe, David W. 2004. *How Sweet the Sound: Music in the Spiritual Lives of Americans*. Cambridge, Mass.: Harvard University Press.

Sundkler, Bengt Gustaf Malcolm. 1961. *Bantu Prophets in South Africa*. London: Lutterworth Press; 1st ed, 1948.

———.1980. *Bara Bukoba: Church and Community in Tanzania*. London: C. Hurst.

Sundkler, Bengt, and Christopher Steed. 2000. *A History of the Church in Africa*. Cambridge: Cambridge University Press.

Suret-Canale, Jean. 1977. *Afrique Noire: L'ère coloniale, 1900–1945*. Paris: Editions sociales.

Taylor, John V. 1963. *The Primal Vision: Christian Presence amid African Religion*. London: SCM Press.

Temu, A. J. 1972. *British Protestant Missions*. London: Longman.

Thiong'o, James Ngugi wa. 1965. *The River Between*. London. Heinemann.

Titon, Jeff Todd, ed. 2002. *Worlds of Music: An Introduction to the Music of the World's Peoples*, 4th ed. Belmont, Calif: Wadsworth.

Turnbull, Colin M. 1968. *The Forest People*. New York: Simon & Schuster.

Turner, Harold W. 1963. "Classification and Nomenclature of Modern African Religious Groups." In *African Independent Church Movements*. Edited by V. E. W. Hayward, 13. London: Edinburgh House Press.

———. 1967a. "A Typology of Modern African Religious Movements," *Journal of Religion and Religions* 1 (1): 1–34.

———. 1967b. "A Typology for African Religious Movements," *Journal of Religion in Africa* 1: 18–21.

———. 1967c. *African Independent Church*, vol. 2. Oxford: Clarendon.

United Nations Educational, Scientific, and Cultural Organization (UNESCO). 2005. http://stats.uis.unesco.org/unesco/TableViewer/tableView.aspx?ReportId=201. Accessed June 21, 2007.

Van Engen, Charles E. 2006a. "Critical Theologizing: Knowing God in Multiple Global and Local Contexts." In *Evangelical, Ecumenical and Anabaptist Missiologies in Conversation*. Edited by James R. Krabill, Walter Sawatsky, and Charles R. Van Engen, 88–98. Maryknoll, N.Y.: Orbis Books.

———. 2006b. "Toward a Contextually Appropriate Methodology in Mission Theology." In *Appropriate Christianity*. Edited by C. H. Kraft, 203–25. Pasadena, Calif.: William Carey Library.

Volz, Carl. 1997. *The Medieval Church*. Nashville: Abingdon Press.

Wachsmann, Klaus P., Erich M. von Honbostel, and Curt Sachs. 1980. "Instruments, Classification of." In *New Grove Dictionary of Music and Musicians*. Edited by Stanley Sadie, 9: 237–45. London: Macmillan Press.

Wagner, Gunther. 1949/1970. *The Bantu of Western Kenya: With Special Reference to the Vugusu and Logoli*. London: Oxford University Press.

Wallace, W. J. 1962. "Hymns in Ethiopia." *Practical Anthropology* 9: 271.

Wallaschek, Richard. 1983. *Primitive Music: an Inquiry into the Origin and Development of Music, Songs, Instruments, Dances and Pantomimes of Savage Races*. London: Longmans, Green.

Walls, Andrew F. 1996. *The Missionary Movement in Christian History: Studies in the Transmission of Faith*. Maryknoll, N.Y.: Orbis Books.

Warnock, Paul Willard. 1983. "Trends in African Church Music: A Historical Review." M.A. thesis, University of California, Los Angeles.

Welbourn, F. B., and B. A. Ogot. 1966. *A Place to Feel at Home: A Study of Two Independent Churches in Western Kenya*. London: Oxford University Press.

Weman, Henry. 1960. *African Music and the Church in Africa*. Vol. 3 of Studia Missionalia Upsaliensia. Uppsala: Svenska Institutet För Missionsforkning.

Wilson-Dickson, Andrew. 1996. *The Story of Christian Music: From Gregorian Chant to Black Gospel An Illustrated Guide to All the Major Traditions of Music in Worship*. Minneapolis: Fortress Press.

World Christian Database. 2007. http://www.worldchristiandatabase.org/wcd/esweb.asp?WCI=Results&Query=415. Accessed June 22, 2007.

World Christian Encyclopedia, 2001. 2nd ed., vol. 1. New York: Oxford University Press.

Glossary

Aerophones: Sound generated from an instrument by vibrating an air column.

Afrocentric: A position founded on a perceived African culture or African worldview.

African Independent Churches (AICs): Historical break-off groups that went "independent" from Western missionary efforts. AICs have served as a reference to African indigenous churches, African instituted churches, African initiated churches, and even, African immigrant churches (i.e., churches of African origin located outside of the continent, mostly in Europe and North America).

Afrogenic: Emanating from, or born in, an African ideology, land, or person.

Aladura groups: African instituted prophet-healing movements which focus on fervent prayer and have developed their own indigenous hymnody. These groups are mostly of Nigerian origin. *Aladura* is a Yoruba word which means "owners of prayer."

Anglophone: From a country that was colonized by the British.

Animistic worship: The worship of spirits in bodies of water, (i.e. ponds), rocks, trees, and inanimate objects through sacrificial offerings of animals, grains, or various libations.

Anglophone Africa: Those parts of Africa that were originally colonized by Great Britain and now speak English as one of the national languages.

Antiphonal: A type of call-and-response pattern where an ensemble is divided into distinct groups performing in alternating turns, sometimes in equal oppostiion.

Balafon: The generic term for a wood frame xylophone found throughout West Africa, and its literal meaning is "the wood that speaks."

Call-and-response form: A form in which a lead singer calls out a musical statement with a group of singers responding to the call. The format varies from simple imitation to highly complex overlapping and interdependent singing of phrases.

Cebaara people: One of thirteen Senari-speaking ethnic Senufo people of West Africa.

Chordophones: Sound generated from an instrument by vibrating a string.

Contextualization: The process of bringing the Christian message into a particular context that makes it understandable by drawing on the cultural gifts of a people as the means of expression.

Creative contextualization: Contextualization done through the use of culturally appropriate art forms, (i.e. music, dance, drama, proverbs, storytelling, and poetry).

Culture: Integrated systems of ideas, feelings, and values with associated patterns of human behavior and products shared by a group of people for organizing and regulating what they think, feel, and do.

Culture area: A concept that classifies ethnic groups according to shared geographical, linguistic, and dominant cultural traits.

Culturally appropriate: Forms and cultural patterns that are drawn from the culture and thus appropriate to it.

Embellishments: Decorations that make something more beautiful.

Ethnomusicology: Originally known as comparative musicology, it is a musicology that includes the study of music in culture and music as culture in all world contexts.

Eulogies: A speech or piece of writing containing high praise of a person, usually a deceased person.

Eurocentric: A position rooted in perceived European culture or European worldview.

Eurogenic: Emanating from, or born in a European ideology, land, or person.

Evangelical Pentecostal Churches: Characteristics of these churches (sometimes also referred to as Charismatic/Pentecostal churches) include some of the classic manifestations of spiritual gifts (e.g., speaking in tongues, prophesy, and so on), a Bible-centered faith, considerable evangelistic zeal, and an energetic style of worship. Many members of these churches tend to think of themselves as less syncretistic than their counterparts in the African initiated churches and more spiritual than those in the Western mission initiated churches.

Francophone: From a country that was colonized by the French.

Francophone Africa: Those parts of Africa that were originally colonized by France and now speak French as one of their national languages.

Global music: All music that occurs around the world.

Gospel: Generic commercial term used in many places in English-speaking Africa for all Christian religious music.

Gospel songs: Originally Christian songs that expressed people's experience of knowing God, especially in light of sin, grace, and temptation. That is, they expressed the Good News of Jesus Christ.

Hermeneutics: The art of interpreting the Bible.

Hermeneutical new song fellowship: Groups of Christians who come together to compose scripture-based songs by studying and interpreting the Bible together and then composing a song on the basis of what has been discussed.

Hymnody: A collection of Christian hymns, often refers to large collections of hymns (i.e., Anglican hymns or Moravian hymns).

Idiophones: Sound generated from an instrument by vibrating the instrument itself.

Indigenous: Objects, cultural products, languages, and people with origins in particular location(s).

Indigenous hymnody: A set of hymns based on the cultural music system of a particular ethnic group of people.

Lamellaphones: Idiophones in which a key (lamella) made of wood or metal is plucked to produce sound. The key itself vibrates.

Lyrics: The words of a song.

Makwaya: Literally, of choirs; it may mean a group of people or an arrangement in choir style.

Malevolent: Having or showing a wish to cause evil or harm to others.

Medieval: A period in the life of humanity also called the Middle Ages.

Membranophones: Sound generated from an instrument by vibrating a stretched skin.

Modal settings: Diatonic scales that derive their characteristic sound from the starting pitch, such as various minor scales depending on where the half-step occurs.

Missiology: The study of doing mission based on conscious, intentional, and ongoing reflection that includes the study and teaching of mission, theories of mission, research, writing, and publication of works about mission.

Monolingual: A person who speaks only one language.

Music-culture: All the ways that a group of people are involved with music, including ideas, actions, institutions, and material objects such as instruments.

Musicking: A coin termed by Christopher Small in 1998 that has gained wide acceptance as definitive of music not just as a product (a noun) but also a process (a verb). Its employment embraces the concept and definition of music beyond Eurocentric parameters of sound—to sounding, visuals and seeing, motor, and feeling. It also refers to participation in music through performance, listening, rehearsal, practice, composition, or movement.

Musical ethnocentrism: The state of being so centered on one's own music that there is no recognition or respect for other people's music.

Musicology: The academic, scholarly study of music.

Narrative songs: Songs that recount a story.

New Religious Movements: This term is used to describe the entire gamut of rapidly flourishing religious groups in Africa, ranging from Christo-centric, Bible-based indigenous churches, to movements marginally shaped and influenced by their encounter with Christianity but which are much closer in intent, belief, and practice to pre-Christian traditional religions. Also known as neo-traditional, synethetist, and hebraist.

Nonliterate: People who have not learned to read or who choose not to read.

Nyarafolo people: One of thirteen Senari-speaking ethnic Senufo people of West Africa.

Orality: Communication patterns that function without the aid of written materials. Oral learners are highly relational, preferring face-to-face communication that specializes in using stories, proverbs, drama, songs, chants, and poetry in communal, participative, and interactive events.

Oral theology: Theological statements and assertions embedded in songs, stories, proverbs, drama, chants, and poetry.

Oral tradition: Communication patterns that function without the aid of written materials, involving stories, proverbs, drama, songs, chants, and poetry.

Pambio: Kiswahili word meaning choruses or refrain.

Parable: A story (usually in the Bible) told to illustrate a moral or spiritual truth.

Pedagogy: Methods and styles of teaching.

Praise and worship: Term used to describe the sung section of a Christian worship service or devotional time particularly in nonliturgical, charistmatic, or Pentecostal groups. It is also a subgenre of gospel music.

Senufo peoples: A West-African ethnic grouping of peoples that spans the north of Côte d'Ivoire, southeast Mali, the southwestern region of Burkina Faso, and along the Ghana-Côte d'Ivoire border. The Senari language is a member of the Voltaic subgroup of the Niger-Congo family that comprises a grouping of thirteen distinct languages.

Spiritual formation: The process of growing spiritually and becoming more Christlike in the Christian faith, commonly referred to as discipleship.

Sub-Saharan Africa: Africa south of the Sahara.

Syncretism: Combination of different philosophical or religious systems of belief or practice. In the case of music in Africa and its use in these concepts, this references the fusion of Afrogenic and Eurogenic musical ideals believed to be different and incompatible.

Taarabu: A music genre found in Eastern, South Eastern, and Central Africa that is founded on Arabic or Arabized music and instruments in fusion with Indic and African ones. Different taarabu subgenres are distinguished by local ethnic and national elements. Most taarabu is performed in the Kiswahili language.

Uhuru: Kiswahili word meaning independence, freedom, liberty, and free will. Associated with the Kenyan movement in the 1950s that sought independence from Great Britain.

Ululation: A singing technique in which a piercing cry is shaped either by the tongue or the uvula. It can signify different things according to the people group using it (i.e., extreme joy or excitement, let's increase the intensity of the song, and so on).

Vernacularization: A language spoken in a particular country or region or by a particular group, also referred to as indigenous language.

Victorian Era: Commonly refers to Queen Victoria's rule in Great Britain between 1837 and 1901.

Western Mission Initiated Churches (WMICs): These historic churches of European and North American origin (e.g., Roman Catholic, Lutheran, Presbyterian, Reformed, Anglican, Baptist, Methodist, independent/nondenominational, and such) make up the majority of the Christian population in sub-Saharan Africa. Their story has intersected in most cases with the history of the European colonial empire on the continent. These churches are the longest-standing and most visible vestige of the encounter between Western Christianity and the precolonial religious traditions of Africa.

Worldview: Cultural ways of looking at life that consists of assumptions, values, and beliefs about what is real, how things fit together, and how things happen by a particular ethnic group, tribe, or nation.

Worship team: Two or more persons leading praise and worship. They can be vocalists, instrumentalists, or both.

List of Contributors

Roberta R. King is currently associate professor of communication and ethnomusicology at Fuller Theological Seminary in Pasadena, California. King oversees and teaches in the global Christian worship (ethnomusicology) program in which students grapple with issues in music, culture, and the church for cross-cultural worship and witness. Her research interests are in ethnomusicology, African music, African music in the church, missiology, and intercultural communication with specialization in the interface between music and communication in global and local contexts of the church. Trained as a choir director, church pianist, and organist, she also plays French horn and is currently singing in a local church choir. In Africa, she has done extensive fieldwork among the Senufo peoples of Côte d'Ivoire and has worked, taught, and ministered in Senegal, Mali, Ghana, the Democratic Republic of Congo, Uganda, and across Kenya. Based in Nairobi, Kenya, for twenty-two years, she founded the department of Christian music communication at Daystar University and also directed the sixty-five-voice choir at Nairobi Baptist Church where she encouraged the use of African musical forms for worship. A missionary pioneer in ethnomusicology with WorldVenture, she has not only ministered extensively across Africa but also taught in parts of Asia and Eastern Europe. Her publications include "Singing the Lord's Song in a Global World" in *Evangelical Missions Quarterly*; "Variations on a Theme of Appropriate Contextualization: Music Lessons from Africa" in *Appropriate Christianity*; "Toward a

Discipline of Christian Ethnomusicology: A Missiological Paradigm" in *Missiology*; *A Time to Sing: A Manual for the African Church*; and *Pathways in Christian Music Communication: The Case of the Senufo of Côte d'Ivoire* (forthcoming).

Jean Ngoya Kidula is currently associate professor of music at the University of Georgia in Athens, Georgia. Kidula's teaching and scholarship are in ethnomusicology with a specialization in the music of Africa, and even more specifically, religious, ritual, and popular music and music in the African Church and the African Academy. Apart from her academic involvement, Kidula is active as a singer, pianist, worship seminar coordinator and conductor both in the United States, Kenya, Tanzania, and Sweden. Before her U.S. employment, Kidula was the music director at the Nairobi Pentecostal church where she oversaw the weekly choral activities and the yearly musical productions. She was also a member of several singing groups as a singer, pianist, guitarist, composer, and arranger of works, ranging from indigenous and national Kenyan folk, classical, and Christian religious to international classical, religious, and gospel styles. She also taught European music theory, history, voice, and piano performance as well as African dance at Kenyatta University in Nairobi, Kenya. Kidula is active as a presenter in conferences and seminars. Her publications in journals and books include such works as "Ethnomusicology, the Music Canon and African Music: Positions, Tensions and Resolutions in the African Academy" in *Africa Today*; "Polishing the Luster of the Stars: Music Professionalism made Workable in Kenya" in *Ethnomusicology*; "African Women Musicians and Music Educators: Catalysts and Culture Brokers" in *African Women and Globalization*; "Christian Music as Indigenous African: Appropriation and Accommodation" in *Multiple Interpretations of Dynamics and Knowledge in African Music Traditions: A Festschrift in Honor of Akin Euba*; and "The Gospel of Andrae Crouch: A Black Angelino" in *California Soul: Music of African Americans of the West*.

James R. Krabill is senior executive for global ministries at Mennonite Mission Network in Elkhart, Indiana. For fourteen years, he served in West Africa, primarily the Côte d'Ivoire, with Mennonite Board of Missions as a Bible and church history teacher among African initiated churches in various village settings, Bible institutes, and theological faculties. For eight of those years, Krabill lived and worked with members of the Harrist Church among Côte d'Ivoire's Dida people, collecting, recording, transcribing, and publishing over five hundred original Harrist hymns for use in literacy and music training. Many of these hymns appeared in two of Krabill's publications, "Dida Harrist Hymnody (1913–1990)" in *Journal of Religion in Africa* and *The Hymnody of the Harrist Church among the Dida of South-Central Ivory Coast*. Krabill is a frequent speaker in various church and academic settings across the United States and has lectured or taught courses in over a dozen countries, most recently at the Bienenberg Centre de Formation et de Rencontre in Switzerland, Irish School of Ecumenics in Ireland, Associated Mennonite Biblical Seminary in Indiana, and Fuller Theological Seminary in California. Krabill is the editor of *Missio Dei*, a quarterly missiological journal, and has authored or edited numerous other books and articles, including, "Scripture Use in AIC Hymnody" in *Afro-Christian Religion at the Grassroots in Southern Africa; Nos racines racontées; Is It Insensitive to Share Your Faith?*; and *Evangelical, Ecumenical and Anabaptist Missiologies in Conversation* with Walter Sawatsky and Charles van Engen.

Thomas Oduro is currently the president of the Good News Theological College and Seminary, in Accra, Ghana. He graduated with a Ph.D. in the history of Christianity from Luther Seminary in Minnesota in 2004. Before that he was awarded a master's degree in systematic theology at the same seminary. He has been a chorister and a choir director in the Church of the Lord (Brotherhood), an African Independent Church, and Calvary Baptist Church, Accra, Ghana. A composer of gospel music, he has run and facilitated many choral music workshops for church choirs in many African independent churches. His interest in church music is the integration of evangelical theology in the composition of songs and historical interplay in the various Christian communities in Africa. His publications include, "Theological Education and Training: Challenges of African Independent Churches in Ghana" in *Journal of African Instituted Church Theology; Catechism for Today: 130 Questions and Answers on What Christians Believe;* and *Christ Holy Church International: The Story of an African Independent Church* (forthcoming).

Index